WHAT IS LIFE?

WHAT IS LIFE?

Reclaiming the Black Blues Self

KALAMU YA SALAAM

Third World Press • Chicago, IL

What Is Life?

Copyright © 1994 Kalamu ya Salaam

Published by Third World Press
P.O. Box 19730
Chicago, IL 60619

ISBN: 0-88378-083-6

Library of Congress Number: 92-63014

Cover Photo by Hughes Jones

Cover Art by Louise Mouton

Cover Design by Angelo Williams

Manufactured in the United States

94 95 96 97 98 99   8 7 6 5 4 3 2 1

this book is dedicated to the Salaam siblings:

Asante Salaam
Mtume ya Salaam
Kiini Ibura Salaam
Tutashinda Nchi na Salaam
Tiaji Jitihadi kwa Salaam

may all of you contribute to the ongoing struggle for peace and liberation for african americans & people of african descent worldwide.

STAY STRONG / BE BOLD!
DO YOUR BEST TO MAKE THIS WORLD BETTER AND MORE BEAUTIFUL AS A RESULT OF YOUR PASSING THROUGH.

in love & struggle
understanding & unity,

Baba
Kalamu ya Salaam

CONTENTS

Introduction

WHAT IS LIFE? / & the beat goes on

What is Life is a book of reflections. It is a culling of essays written since 1983 and poems written since 1980. For the most part, this book excludes most of the cultural criticism and music-related pieces that made up the bulk of my writing during this period. What is here is a lot of stuff I have thought about in the midnight hours.

Third World Press has presented me with the opportunity to share the introspective and probing pieces that grapple with the "what am I here for?" and "what did I do to be so black & blue?" questions of life, which all of us, to one degree or another, struggle to answer.

This collection would not be a reality were it not for the patient but persistent encouragement and assistance of my initial editor, Donna Williams. We have wrestled with this manuscript for almost two years. In the interim, other projects have been completed. Were I left to my own initiative, I probably would have let *What Is Life* pass, as I have a propensity to move on. There are literally five or six other books in various stages of completion which would have had all of my attention had not Donna stayed on me to complete the corrections and adjustments for *What Is Life*. My second editor, Bakari Kitwana helped me to shape the final structure of the book, creating a consistent style. Asante sana (thank you very much) to both of them.

This book is written from the most emotionally taxing decade I had ever endured: the 80s. The Civil Rights (mid-50s to mid-60s) and Black Liberation Struggle (mid-60s thru the 70s) years were certainly very difficult and very dangerous, but they were also very exhilarating and inspiring. The 80s were torture. We spent the preceding three decades on the battlefield. The 80s were spent in captivity.

The title for this collection comes from a period in my life when I was asking myself a lot of detailed questions. This was a period of emotional transition that followed the 1985 break-up of a sixteen year-old marriage. In 1987, shortly after this break-up, I had resigned from what many in New Orleans considered to be one of the best jobs available as the executive director of the New Orleans Jazz & Heritage

Foundation (the parent organization of the famous New Orleans Jazz & Heritage Festival).

With five children beginning to move into college, I knew that it seemed highly irrational for me to be moving away from emotionally and financially secure situations into uncertainties, but move I did. Also, I was grappling with the exhaustion of our Pan-African Nationalist organization, Ahidiana, which had consumed a major portion of my adult life (1973 - 1983). That same year (1983), I left the *Black Collegian Magazine*, where I had been a founding member and editor for thirteen years. All in all, on paper, it seems bizarre. But obviously, these were moves I deeply felt I had to make.

While I have accomplished a lot in the intervening years, particularly in the areas of music production, creative writing, and fiction, little of that (except for the poetry) is reflected in this collection. What is here are my philosophical concerns: how racism, economic exploitation, sexism, and heterosexism interconnect and complicate the age-old questions of being and self-definition. This is an honest sharing of what has been happening with me. From what I can see, these issues have also affected a lot of other people of my generation.

The poetry included here covers a broader range of years but essentially maps the same or similar concerns. In general, I do not date my writing, but essentially what is included here is poetry of the 80s with a few pieces written after 1990. I include the poems because many of them are what I call "sun songs," sermon-like, performance pieces that wrestle with hard facts of life and hope to inspire deeds. The two main stylistic inspirations are: (1) great Black music, especially jazz; and (2) the oratory of Baptist preachers.

I was born 24 March 1947, came of age in the Civil Rights Movement and was an active adult during the Black Power struggles of the 70s. Needless to say, I have had to wrestle with the demons of depression during the 80s, and am now trying to construct a realistic and effective ideology to serve my continuing development. These essays are a spirit-gram, mapping the currents of my mind while zooming through the last days/years of the 20th century. I do not claim to be a prophet or even a political analyst. Simply put, I'm an African American man trying hard to live up to my fullest potential—to do my best to contribute to the empowerment of my people and the betterment and beautification of the whole world—in my own space and time.

WHAT IS LIFE?

Reclaiming the Black Blues Self

INSIDE:

the lyric/song of love

Sun Song I

blues zephyr

that man with the whole of doo-wop
in his head entered through his blk eye
spying the significance of all he's seen, a
wild-haired head that manages without haircut, a
head where few would expect beauty to reside, a
head where pain has a permanent box
& receives mail everyday, that
man

that man with the wrinkled khaki trousers
no cleaners will ever see & the odor
of no job in the morning clinging like sweaty
shirt, that
man

that man languidly leaning against liquor
store wall, who won't hesitate to wolf
whistle behind a pretty woman or silently
stare down an approaching cop car without
flinching a facial muscle, that
man

that man soul serenaded yesterday's twilight
for no reason other than that's what he felt
like doing, singing, in a clear, high falsetto,

enthralling our decaying neighborhood with an arcing
improvised shoo-bee-do which momentarily
suspended the march of time, that
man

when that man finished singing to the newly
risen moon, all any of the enviously staring
others of us could do was amen in chorus
when walter admiringly shouted out to that
man

"go on, cool breeze
you know you bad"

the blues aesthetic

recognized or not, blues people manifest a blues sensibility, a post-reconstruction expression of peoplehood culturally codified into an aesthetic. lest we be terribly mistaken, we must understand two factors: (1) not all african americans are blues people, and (2) the blues aesthetic is an ethos of blues people that manifests itself in everything done, not just in the music.

maybe the easiest way to define the blues (and by extension, the blues aesthetic) is to define what it ain't.

the blues ain't slave music. didn't no slaves sing the blues.* we didn't become blue until after reconstruction, after freedom day and the dashing of all hopes of receiving/attaining our promised 40acres&1mule. in essence, the blues aesthetic is the cultural manifestation of former slaves expelled from the land, promised a new land, and ultimately and callously, turned into an easily exploitable surplus, unskilled and semi-skilled, migratory, landless, politically unenfranchised labor pool. even when we left the plantations under what we thought was our own steam, it was really an expulsion from the slave agrarian/plantation society into the emerging urban/industrial society. our so-called great migration should be seen specifically for what it was: mass urbanization.

---

* cf. *looking up at down, the emergence of blues culture* by william barlow (temple u. press) for a good general history on the blues as a music form.

this social process, this dispossession of the formerly possessed, set the stage for the two basic blues music forms, country and urban. in this case, the labels accurately say it all. on the plantation, our enslaved ancestors sang work songs, field hollers, chants, remembered and retained african songs (often in a transformed state), colored variations of euro-centric music, but not no blues. we first got the blues on the southern roads moving from work camp to work camp, farm to town, town to city, and then, in the slaughter houses and firestorm ovens of the mills & foundries of the cities, both down- and up-south.

the blues is not african. samuel charters dedicated many years trying to chase down the african roots of the blues. the savannaheat laughed at him. bits and pieces of pre-blues forms floating in the night were carried to his ear on the wind, but he never found the song, not to mention the singer. although certain african elements (including scales and instrumental/ vocal techniques) are undeniable, west africa simply did not have the social basis to give rise to a blues vision. west african colonialism, although far from culturally benign, wasn't even a sound check compared to the magic act of how africans became negroes in the u.s.a. melting pot. some of us, out of a real ignorance of what went down, underestimate the transformative force of slavery, civil war, reconstruction, and jim crow, but we ignore this unique historical development at the cost of rendering all our theories about black folk, blues aesthetic, etc., null and totally void.

no other people, except african americans created the blues, not even other africans enslaved other places in the western hemisphere. other african peoples in the western hemisphere went from agrarian slavery to some strained and, of course, de facto fraudulent form of urban industrial integration. these other forms of urban integration generally lacked the obsessive racial segregation shown out in 99% of america. the strange (in american terms) racial reality and climate of black-creole-white/english&french new orleans, vis-a-vis the rest of white-black/english speaking america offers a home-grown comparison of caribbean and american racial mores, and demonstrates our thesis about the difference between african americans in the u.s.a. and blacks elsewhere in the western hemisphere.

some day we will speak on the puritanism of the north combining with the racialism of the south and the effect of this combination on blues people, but, at this juncture, we simply note that any objective reading of comparative history will document that the u.s.a. invented apartheid under the rubric of national democracy with social segregation. today, there remains a link between 20th-century black south african culture and african american blues culture. the similarities are more than surface: apartheid is nothing but the logical progression of racially based economic exploitation (u.s.a.: slavery -> share-cropping and segregation / south africa: colonialism -> apart-heid) facilitated, in both cases, by the rapid change of an agrarian-based society into an industrial/urban society.

while i am fully aware there are other factors, those factors supplement but do not substitute for the economic/political basis. economics and politics do not always take the lead. however, the basic shape of america was enforced by those who put economics and politics in the lead. for those conquerors, racial genocide and racism seemed sensible, logical and a mandate from god—the same god who had blessed these christians with the wisdom and strength to conqueror the savage red & black pagans.

within that context, it is obvious that what we are dealing with is more than solely a music form or aesthetic, although it is mainly in the musical form that the blues aesthetic has most often been recognized by non-blues people. the comparative uniqueness of this music is impossible to confuse or mis-classify, especially when heard in juxtaposition to any euro-centric music. however, the mere thought that the blues is mainly music is a grossly euro-centric misconception. this misconception is based partially on an inability to perceive african americans as having a self-defined total culture that includes abstract aesthetical considerations, mundane manifestations in everyday life, and classical manifestations in archetypal artistic creations.

recognized or not, blues people manifest a blues sensibility. after two or three generations, that manifestation has been culturally codified into an aesthetic that shows out in everything done, not just in the music. however, non-african american observers of african american culture find it difficult to recognize anything but the music. african american culture in general, and blues culture in particular, is literally a mystery to most americans. this mystery approaches roughly the same level as ancient egyptian sacred architecture and dogonian cosmic worldviews, both of which are far more hip than the average, american university in both physical representation and philosophical essence.

if i were to describe the blues aesthetic in culturally consistent terms, i would wittily use a metaphor: the blues is like running a downtown, no-trump boston when life has dealt you nothing but low cards. and we all know bid whist is a game of chance, daring, improvisation, and skill all rolled into one. in contrast, bridge is a game in which bidding skill and strategy minimize the chance distribution of the cards.

our people's aesthetic, post-reconstruction and pre-civil rights, evolved out of our dealing with the hand life dealt us. that hand was generally disappointing and usually negatively disproportionate in its distribution of winners. anything that individuals do, if it reflects their peoplehood, is best understood as both an individual and a representative act. these acts usually reflect the day-to-day living conditions of that people. culture, despite our public school education's position, is not the story of how great individuals created specific aesthetics (& artifacts) and/or ideologies (& social systems). we people of color prefer aesthetics to ideology. life is more interesting and fulfilling that way, thank you.

the end of african american mass espousal of the blues aesthetic was marked by the wholesale acceptance of integration and the concurrent destruction of our working-class economy. after reconstruction, we developed a goods and services infrastructure that lasted until we abandoned being and developing ourselves for the (dis)illusion of being and developing ourselves into others (an other that was often antithetical to the blues self). but as with any good dialectic, in the process of moving toward and becoming like the other, our contact with the other also moved the others toward becoming like us. in fact, the very elements in the euro-centric community who were attracted to blues people were those who often represented the repressed currents of europe, which were often branded as primitive and/or permissive.*

---

* it is no accident that the social background of whites who are heavy into the blues mainly includes jews, appalachian dispossessed drifters, 2nd/3rd—generation eastern european descendants, and whites who philosophically gravitated toward non-christian currents of european thought.

unlike slavery, segregation did not rule out the development of a black-controlled indigenous economy peopled in the
main by black professionals and artisans. this economy
provided the base for african american society as a whole and
was glued together by our people's general desire for self-
improvement. the political vector of this call was expressed via
marcus garvey's unia—a blues organization, if you will. the unia
was really more blues (although it called itself "negro") than
african, notwithstanding the fact that it was quickly dubbed a
"back-to-africa" movement, a natural categorization. wasn't no
integrationists going to be even thinking (either figuratively,
aesthetically, or literally) about going back to africa. witness:
non-blues-based harlem renaissance poets literally and psychologically re-crossed the atlantic but turned north instead of
south. they took boat rides to europe (most often to paris),
where the jazz age was in vogue and the cubists had discovered
africa. these negro wannabe poets ran to study "real" culture
from artists who themselves were busy studying africa and were
attracted to sophisticated and/or authentic africans. (talk about
contradictions within contradictions!) fortunately, pathology
is a different discipline from aesthetics.

there are a number of central elements of the blues
aesthetic and likewise a number of key manifestations of it.
listed below is a condensed and simplified codification of the
blues aesthetic:

1. *stylization of process*—i.e., whatever blues people did,
   it was done with a style that emphasized the collective
   tastes and simultaneously demonstrated the individual variation on the collective statement. this
   practice, of course, is based on call/response motifs
   but might more accurately be identified as theme/

variation. if you know the history of the music, the use of theme/variation marked the movement from agrarian (communal) forms to urban (collective) forms. the communal form required the audience. in the collective form, the artists became their own audience, and the audience moved from communal participant to observer of the collective, from proactive participant to quasi-passive observer, from ritual to entertainment. of course, none of this is absolute. nevertheless, there was a shift that can be stylistically traced through the music.

2. *the deliberate use of exaggeration* to call attention to key qualities, with wit being one of the most salient projections of exaggeration. humor is essentially nothing but an exaggeration of reality in order to make a point. (ever wonder why some people miss a joke that is really obvious? if you don't know the reality, you can't appreciate the joke, precisely because the joke is a comment on the reality.)

3. *brutal honesty clothed in metaphorical grace*, which included at its core a profound recognition of the economic inequality and political racism of america. at the same time, this honesty is clothed in a profound appreciation of the fact that every strength got a weakness and that it is better to recognize (and sometimes even ridicule) rather than cover up weaknesses.

4. *acceptance of the contradictory nature of life*—life is both

sweet and sour. while generally you got a pot of the latter, almost everybody is guaranteed at least a spoonful of the former. here one must be careful not to confuse dualism with dialectics. life is not about good vs. evil, but about good and evil eaten off the same plate.

5. *an optimistic faith in the ultimate triumph of justice* in the form of karma. what is wrong will be righted. what is last will be first. balance will be brought back into the world. this faith was often co-opted by christianity, but is essential even to the most down-trodden of the blues songs.

6. *celebration of the sensual and erotic* elements of life, as in "shake it but don't break it!"

let us suggest a little deeper investigation of these central elements of the blues aesthetic. as with any culture in the world, those who projected a blues culture did so first of all through a stylization of process. the blues process, afro-centric to the core, simultaneously emphasizes the collective tastes of the community while at the same time encourages, indeed often demands, individual variations on the collective statement. as stated above, this pattern is clearly seen as call/response, but is more accurately understood as theme/variation.

stylization of process can be noted in any activity in which a group of blues people participate, e.g., soldiers marching in drill: check how african american soldiers turn close-order drill into dance, listen to how they call cadence, follow their syncopated shuffle-step variations on the basic martial march. this synchronization of individual variation within a communal framework is the single most identifiable characteristic of the blues culture. it is a characteristic that achieves the maximizing of both the community and the individual while avoiding the negation of either. this same dance pattern, without evident music, manifests itself in black greek fraternity and sorority step lines.*

those who were raised on the euro-centric concept of objectivity (so-called) and its visual corollary, "proper perspective," immediately notice and often condemn the afro-centric blues worldview which makes deliberate use of exaggeration to call attention to key qualities (i.e., qualities to be upheld or dismissed, the hip or the triflin'. the ordinary is, of course, beneath contempt). in this context, wit, sarcasm, and irony are salient expressions of exaggeration, since humor is essentially nothing but an exaggeration of reality in order to make a point. another example of exaggeration is how we wear clothes. the ace-deuced angularity off the x-y axis that we choose to use when we profile in our sky pieces (i.e., the way we wear hats) is by now legendary. we also manifest exaggeration with color combinations as well as the cut and drape of the cloth. hence, the fashion visuals of rappers and other popular entertainers (such as m.c. hammer) is nothing but a late 20th-century manifestation of the african american zoot suit mentality/ modality.

as parliament/funkadelic has cogently stated, the beautiful thing abt our blues-based fantasies is that they are alternative visions to what exists in our world. we act out these visions with style. so rather than an escape from reality, when we fantasize, it is based on a brutally honest recognition of reality, a reality

---

* zora neale hurston's "characteristics of negro expression" is a seminal essay in this regard.

albeit clothed in metaphorical grace. this grace includes, but is not overcome by, a profound recognition of the economic inequality and political racism of america. thus, we laugh loud and heartily when every rational expectation suggests we should be crying in despair. the combination of exaggeration and conscious recognition of the brutal facts of life is the basis for the humor of blues people, which is real black humor. when we be being funny among ourselves and not to amuse or entertain others, then you had better be prepared to deal with some brutal honesty. this brutalness is most often packaged in irony supreme. comedian richard pryor aptly illustrates, indeed embodies, both brutal honesty when dealing from and to blues people as well as self-deprecation and self-negation when acting like a silly commercial entertainer. just to indicate one thread: richard pryor is sexuality-active when he is on a blues vibe, whereas, when he is on an entertainment tip, he is a eunuch or else slavishly conforms to mainstream, wasp, white, sexual behavior.

blues people are not interested in heaven or hell except in so far as those locales are manifested in the here and now. thus, blues people accept the contradictory nature of life. life is once again, both sweet and sour, rather than one or the other. while generally you catch a whole lot of hell, almost everybody is guaranteed at least a spoonful of heaven. here one must be careful not to confuse dualism with dialectics. life is not about heaven vs. hell, but about heaven and hell in each life. this seemingly (although not true) fatalism is leavened by our optimistic faith in the ultimate triumph of justice. again, what is wrong will be righted. what is last will be first. balance will be brought back into the world. this faith was often co-opted by christianity, but is essential even to the most "low-down" of the blues songs.

our optimism is too deep for the average person to understand just by wondering how any one individual survives. in order to accept/understand blues optimism, we need to accept/understand history from the middle passage up through the end of slavery. most of our ancestors would rather have died before accepting slavery. did just that. they died. some died fighting. some committed suicide. those who survived were essentially those who chose to accept the contradictory nature of life and move into the future with an unshakable optimistic faith in the ultimate triumph of justice. optimism among african americans is not just philosophical. five hundred years after the atlantic slave trade started, optimism is also genetic.*

the blues aesthetic is not abstract. while it has an abstract philosophical underpinning, it is celebratory in the here and now, body and soul. this is why the blues aesthetic emphasizes and enjoys the sensual and erotic elements of life. while this is apparent in all our dance, in all our music, in all the delight we take in physical beauty, it has taken us quite a number of centuries to get repressed puritanical peoples to accept that it really is okay to enjoy both the sensual and erotic sides of life. we are not arguing that any of these characteristics are exclusive to blues people, even though, within the context of the u.s.a., it may seem that way. on the other hand, the embracing of this concept by non-african americans sometimes leads to exces- siveness, even obsession, with exotica and an elevation of the other as the paragon of sensuality or sexuality (as in the fixation

---

* a profound run down of the african origins of this view of life (contrasted to the euro-centric tragic view of life) is presented by cheik anta diop in *the cultural unity of black africa.*

on mulatto women). this objectification of people is really a corruption of this basic concept that is essentially about an informed view of one's own sensual and erotic self, rather than an obsession with someone else's sensual and erotic self. a quick survey of western visual arts, including the mapplethorpe visualization of the black male nude, highlights this distinction. the true blues aesthetic locates sensuality and sexuality not in the other but in the self.

hopefully, this brief overview will help us understand the blues aesthetic as an aesthetic which has music at the core, but which also informs and significantly influences every aspect of community life.

the chief cultural manifestations of a blues aesthetic are: (1) country & city blues, (2) jazz, (3) african american fashion, (4) the oral tradition, (5) popular black dance, and (6) african american cuisine.

a brief aside: some say that music is the strongest rather than simply the most well-known manifestation of the blues aesthetic. to the degree that this assertion is true, it is true because music is the least concrete, the most ephemeral and therefore the least subject to inspection and oppression by outside forces. slavery would not allow a blues culture to manifest itself. that is why the blues aesthetic is post-reconstruction. similarly, once a decision was made by the masses to try integrating into the american cultural mainstream, the blues aesthetic ceased to be the dominant mode of cultural expression precisely because it was not like the mainstream. further, it was often anti-mainstream, clashing in values and indices of beauty.

while there are certainly other elements and manifestations, this blues overview will serve to keep our eyes on the prize. also, it will help us to understand why the blues seems to have fallen on hard times. why and when did blues people stop liking the blues? this viewpoint, also, implicitly suggests the value of a blues aesthetic in a post-industrial age. the key question is this: where are the masses of our people headed? that's not an easy question to answer. currently, we are in a period of rapid transition, fissure, and dispersal. we don't even live together as a people. (the forces of integration are centrifugal by nature.)

the integrationists, led by the ultra-corrupt negro politicians who attain status without substance (even when they have some stroke, they generally end up in a masturbatory posture) and the ultra-impotent athlete/entertainer in the show business of sports and entertainment,* are the two most visible categories of nationally recognized, high profile black leaders(?????!!!!!). they have run their version of the american dream road show into the ground. at the same time, the political activists, the nationalists and leftists (two sides of the same coin sometimes), are ideologically bankrupt and devoid of major influence in inner-city america. although there is political struggle going on, it is either very local and lacking a national profile, or else it has no real currency among the masses. thus blues people are in search of a direction. the reason there is so much confusion manifesting itself as criminality and anarchy in the community is because there is no community.

if we ever had the blues (in a simplistic, but not altogether inaccurate, sense), we gots it now. now, more than ever, we need culture to give some direction, and hence, some hope to

---

* black athletes and entertainers are generally nothing more than the "show," often well paid for a brief period, but always expendable for the next two, three, or four-year sports/music icon.

what appears to be a rather hopeless situation.

there is more, but you can't swallow but one mouthful at a time.

Sun Song II

my name is kalamu

I am African-Diaspora
I am ancient and new
I am African-American
I am resistance and assimilation
I am a proud and pure cultural mulatto
I am well-used labor unemployed
I am illiterate intelligence
I am beauty deformed
I am the fuel of Pan-American cultures
I am freedom without wealth
    in my world of constant war
I am a country with no army
I am everyone's love song
    and even though no one wants to be me
    — sometimes not even I —
    with the tender touch of my calloused hand
    I continue tending the fruit and flower garden of me

I am raped human wise enough to nevertheless
    love my woman self, knowing no woman
    survives slavery untouched
I am Tubman feet willfully returning again
    and again to steal my people away
    from thieves
I have killed my children to save them from slavery
I have nursed my children, Black and mulatto,

teaching them all to respect and value life
Who knows the pain of slave pregnancy: nine
      months of growing a baby who will surely
      be beaten down—I know
I have sold myself to save my daughters
      and sons from the defilement of poverty
I have denied myself and extinguished
      my dream candles to light a chance for my children
I have chewed the centuries-old flag of degradation every
      morning and miraculously somehow managed to suck
      small droplets of hope from the warp and woof of filth
      which i transformed into warm milk and
      breastfed to my babies
No woman knows how to love better than I
      — I love strong men and love pieces
      of men, I love all my babies no matter
      the shade of their skin, and even in the deepest
      white night of my despair, I also love myself
I wrap our wounds with the silk-strong softness of my caring
      and the salve cream of my patient quietness hugging
      hurt to the huge humanness of my heart
      knowing that for us, the survivors of slavery,
      there is no better therapy than love and struggle, so
I freely supply the love and steadfastly support the struggle

I am emasculated man collaborating and consciously forgetting
      to emulate Zumbi, Nat Turner & Toussaint
I am self-emancipating man resisting
      with words, with music, with arms
      with whatever, an enduring Mandela of resistance
Sometimes I kill my master and love my brother
Sometimes I kill my brother and love my master
Sometimes I just kill everything
Sometimes I kill nothing
Sometimes I love no one

Sometimes I love everyone
Even I cannot predict how I will feel/
        what I will think
        what day is this?
        what is happening?

Civilization did not birth me
Civilization could not create me
Civilization in enslaving me
        disfigured but ultimately failed
        to totally transform me
They tried conquest and captivity
They expounded dead thinking that stinks
They ceaselessly exploited the strength of my
        labor and shamelessly, in the name of development,
They forged for me an endless debt
They legislated my dependence, my marginalization
        my alienation
They blessed me and so-called saved me
        using all the inhumanity Christian masters
        could stuff into my mouth
But my vomit is beautiful
        my spit is song
        my tears are laughter
Five hundred years of civilization
        and the masses of me still
        will not cut our hair
        shave all our faces
        cover our mouths when we laugh
        or stop making music, love and babies
I am stronger than dirt

But sometimes I am so full of shit
        you can smell me a mile away
        sometimes

sometimes I drink too many "sorry-for-myselfs" on ice
*   or gulp glasses full of warm "we-will-never-wins"*
*   until I reel in a drunken self-depreciating stupor*
sometimes I am irresponsible and despondent
sometimes I give up hope, wear black ties and
*   declare my Blackness should not be noticed*
sometimes I flash diamond rings and do not care
*   that they are stolen teeth*
*   of South African miners, crystallized tears*
*   from Brazilian favelas*
sometimes I act like I am big stuff
*   and demand to be treated like a rich slave*
*   merchant whose only concern for Blackness is how*
*   I can profit*
sometimes I even expertly wield the whip of oppression
*   like some half-human latin american*
*   dictator decored with rows and rows of brutality*
*   medals made of broken bones pinned gloriously*
*   across my puffed-up chest*
or at the very least I aspire to be a u.s. senator
*   smoking a long cigar, drinking rare cognac and laughing*
*   at the donkey fucking the native woman at the private*
*   floor show staged in my honor after I have cut*
*   a deal and sit bloated with pride, unbelievably happy*
*   about the good fortune of my lucrative sell-out*
or is it some monster criminal I admire with big hat,
*   blazing fast guns and cocained realities*
or maybe I'm the infamous international singer with
*   thirty thousand tight dresses, surgically shaped*
*   breasts, a beautiful voice and a string of male*
*   lovers, none of whom look like me*
sometimes I look in the mirror and I am not there
but that invisible self-negation is also me, sometimes

Nevertheless no matter where parts of me may run
  most of me always remains
  barefoot on the ground watching the elite
  be driven over me as they thank
  their new gods that they are no longer me

Although I am sometimes a thing,
  a wild monster grown fat on self-cannibalism, the majority
  of me is a creature of the earth and not an object
  sprung fully formed from the forehead of some great European
In essence I am simply a wonderful being, like so many others
In this world teeming with amazing delights,
  there are so many uncaged birds and happy fish,
  fast multi-colored horses and me
  there are hardwood trees and wispy clouds, wild mountains,
  naked beaches and me
  there are trade winds, gently baked moon illuminations,
  white foaming green waves and me
I am not a creation of men, those
  creations are automobiles and toilet seats
  televisions and rocket ships, cheeseburgers and satellites
Box me in a ship and send me
  to Brazil, still i am me
Tie me in a seat and fly me
  to New York still i am me
Drop me on a burro and walk me
  to Bluefields (in Nica. libre) i remain me
Slow cruise me secretly at night
  from Grenada to Barbados, Antigua
  to St. Kitts, Martinique to Trinidad
  to any of them, to all of them
  what do I become? in essence
  nothing different because the insides
  of all of that is me

no matter the currency or rate of exchange
no matter the longitude or location of our U.N. seat
no matter the year of our abolition
no matter when we first voted
    or who was our first rich man
no matter how many sports games we win
    or how much we are paid to shake our ass
no matter your perception
    or my subjectivity
even as we are cut by colonial customs
    into portuguese pieces, into spanish pieces
    into french pieces and english pieces
no matter in what way each of us
twists their tongue in order to articulate
    our sounds
none of that matters
if I hug you hard and you kiss me sincerely
if I and I music together
    dance samba, play pans
    kiaso, gospel and jazz
if we wage struggle wherever we are
    and enjoy peace in each other's presence
if we laugh at ourselves with each other
    and are serious about helping one another
if i love what you see in me
    and you love what i see in you
if we seek each other's substance
    and eschew each other's shadow
if my liberty is your freedom
    and your equality my upliftment
if my brother is Maurice Bishop
    and your brother is Malcolm X
if this, then what does a name matter?

my name is kalamu,
that is how i am called
but inside the fullness of me I know
my whole name must include all your names,
all the handles you use, indeed
our ancestors sagaciously buffed
our resplendent obsidian inner-spirit walls
preparing us to receive the hieroglyphed history
of our common conditions which chatteled centuries
have etched into each of us, Black
codes mutely detailing, once we learn
to read ourselves, the deep and someday
soon shining joy-soaked futures
we all would love to taste

when we braille-read the keloided past
of us and sight read the as-yet-unformed
future of us, then today's names can be seen
for exactly what they are and no more,
simply little scribbles, just different
little catch phrases conveniently used
to detail specific manifestations of
a talented and multi-textured black experience
whose nucleus is foreign to none of us

when i learn to pronounce your name
i am simply discovering
another me

my name is kalamu

now,
what is yours?
tell me how to speak my name

What is Life?

Death is not life. This, we instinctively know. Inevitably, our time must come. Death will carry us away and, for us, that will be the end of life. Thus, death, by both its finality and inevitability, is a major definer of life.

Death brooks no compromise. Death is the master and will force us to recognize its supremacy. Even before our name is called, whether or not we anticipate death's arrival, death will force us to taste its kiss when it claims one who is close to us—the juice of its pain permanently staining our teeth.

Sometimes death is straight up. You see the sneaky sickle swinging and, emotionally, you shield yourself. But sometimes there is no warning.

You enter a dark house after a long and trying day. You hear noises you ought not hear. Your eyes adjusting, you begin to see. You are not alone. A burglar? The awful stillness of confrontation. The intruder exits through a window on the other side of the house. You turn on the lights. Your stomach turns. Papers and clothing are strew across the floor. Cabinet doors ajar. Drawers hang half- and three-quarters open. Shit.

Just as nothing prepares you to calmly accept the ransacking of your living quarters, nothing prepares you to casually confront death when you don't see it coming.

My mother died of Hodgkin's disease in 1975. She had endured chemotherapy and in the end died with her spirit resplendently unbroken. When her time came, she simply folded her arms and flew away. Two days before her ascension, she called us all to her bedside—my two younger brothers, my father, her siblings, and close friends. She knew. We knew. I was prepared for her death, and her death prepared me for subsequent deaths.

But almost exactly a decade later, after biting into some particularly bitter fruit, I was consciously forced to recognize that not just people die. Organizations die. Relationships die. Suddenly, something you expected to last forever slips away from you.

In human terms, forever is not very long. I am now well into my forties. A friend of mine believes that death is a more pressing reality for us now because we are older and the passing of people we know will happen more and more often. That is true. But, more importantly, these early 90s—like the butt-end years of the 80s—are a killing time. Not simply a time of things falling apart, but indeed, a time of environmental murder.

Though it is natural and understandable that death marks the creation of the past, it is also a bewildering and almost blinding idiosyncrasy of the present that we are building the past faster than we are creating the future. Indeed, in some places in the world today, the death rate is actually higher than the birth rate. Whole species of human and animal life are being wiped out. What we have is zero or negative creative growth in social development and in actual human production.

We cannot drink the river water, the lake water, nor even the rain water in many places. Much of the food we eat is poisoned. The corruption of politics has proliferated so much that its naked corpulence can no longer be camouflaged. Unemployment and bankruptcy dog our footsteps, clinging like the stink of fresh canine excrement into which we have inadvertently stepped.

We are paying the price for our fascination with instant gratification. Plastics have replaced metals; nylons, rayons and other "-ons" have replaced cotton, wool, and leather; appliances that formerly lasted decades now have built-in obsolescence. The list could easily be extended. Has our social and physical environment prepared us to expect and accept a short life span for nearly everything we touch and for everything that touches us, whether human, animal, material, ideological, etc.?

Values don't last (some would add, "like they used to"). Relationships. Tools and toys. Cars and clothes. Nothing lasts, it seems. This not-lasting, however, has a special meaning that we sometimes do not comprehend. Contemporary America is a society with a subconscious death fixation. A few generations back, when something broke you fixed it. Today, you throw it away. Why? Because its usefulness has ended, it is dead, and there is no repair for death. Movies, videos, and television (especially the evening news that daily brings "real" deaths into our private spaces) have all helped trivialize the finality of death. Death watching has become rousing and arousing entertainment.

Contemporary movies amuse us with the fanciful killing of individuals, many of whom "just happen to be in the way." The woman jogging through the park is raped and strangled by an anti-hero who sports a popular brand of running shoe. The camera shows his feet, not his face; what he wears becomes who he is. The elderly man is smashed against a pastel-colored stucco wall by a car during a crashing chase. (These old people are seldom anyone we are led to know. They exist as fragile props to be beaten or mutilated.)

The evening news tell us, in cool non-emotional voices, about real deaths that took place sometime in the last twenty-four hours, somewhere on this vast planet, albeit a time and place accessible by portable camera, suggest that the most human response we can give to distant death is "so what?" How do these deaths affect my paycheck, the value of my property, my relationship with my lover?

When death becomes entertainment, our psyches are sinisterly shaped to submit. While the deaths of relatives, friends, and acquaintances continue to stun us, we become so numbed by popularized death that death takes on an impersonal omnipresence to which we readily acquiesce. I hear Rev. Gary Brown singing "Death don't have no mercy in this land...." No mercy. Our emotional homes have been ransacked. The thieves are stealing our lives, taking pieces of us out the window. Death. Think about it.

* * * * * * * * * *

My reflections on death emerged from events I did not foresee, but events whose impact demanded my full concentration before I could move beyond them. In 1985, I was not simply a witness to a death in which I was personally involved, I became a murderer.* I murdered my marriage. "Murdered" because although I felt too weary to continue the relationship, I was not too weary to willfully put a stop to it. My partner Tayari did not want to end it. I did.

---

* To recognize this was to recognize how "American" I actually am.

Although I had never taken the longevity of my marriage for granted, I never expected the relationship to end. I certainly never envisioned being the one who would walk away from our marriage. But I did, and that walking away both hurt and humbled me. I would lay awake some nights, staring into the darkness and looking at myself. Almost forty years old, I lay stretched out on a bed by a window in the same room where I grew up three decades earlier. But this was thirty years later. I had returned to my father's house. He welcomed me. Never questioned why or how I had arrived. He gave me a lot of space as I wrestled with the eerie notion that my father was not surprised that I left my marriage.

I was hurting, but not out of self-pity or guilt. I am instinctively competitive. I hate to lose. But more than that, I hate to give up. Yet, sometimes life is beyond our control. No matter the popularity of "rugged American individualism," the individual is not lord. The individual, although a powerful force, is limited. The major problem is the invisible fences. Too often we can not see what stops us. Even as we are stymied, even as we are frustrated, we feel it but we can not see it. We can not understand what limits us. What authority? What superior power? In the face of invisibility, sometimes all we can see is our own weakness. Such situations can debilitate you, can take the wind out of you like an unseen cross-body block thrown on you by a crafty opponent as you run full-tilt downfield, your eyes fixed on some distant ball-carrier whom you desire to tackle.

I'd lay in my room hurting. I was overwhelmed by a sense of failure, even as I resolved to call it quits.

I was humbled. I have a high level of self-confidence and firmly believe in self-control and self-determination. I do not believe that I can do anything I want to, but I do believe that

I can do almost anything. But this was something I could not do. I could not work out my relationship with Tayari. Gradually, I came to realize that, as with so many other obstacles in life we fail to overcome, part of my failure was not a failure of ability but a failure of will: I really did not want to do whatever it would have taken to make the relationship work.

In the small room with two windows, the same room I grew up in as a child, I came to the realization that I was ending a major phase of my adult life and embarking on a new phase.

As I looked at it, almost all of the major relationships I had formed in the past had either ended or were downgraded from major to minor. Realizing this, I began to formulate my theory of death as the dominant reality for African Americans in the 80s.

Before the termination of my marriage, I had resigned from Ahidiana, a Pan-African Nationalist organization.* In 1983 I had left the *Black Collegian Magazine*, a publication I had helped to found in 1970. All of these events were milestone markers that turned into tombstones as I ran past them toward the 1990s.

I was born during the post-war optimism of the late 40s, went through puberty on picketlines buoyed by the promise of civil rights in the mid-60s. By the 70s, Black Power in my eye and liberation on my mind, I and many others put all our chips on making momentous change on the mountainous political landscape of America. But mountains, unless blown up, change ever so slowly. We went to the mountain. By the 80s,

---

* Ahidiana was a political formation which had operated a school since its inception in May 1973, a bookstore for about three years, and a printing press/publishing apparatus for five or six years. Ahidiana had organized and instituted cultural programs in New Orleans, such as Kwanzaa, a lecture series, and had participated and initiated community-oriented political activities including anti-apartheid demonstrations.

we discovered that as much as we changed the mountain, the mountain also changed us. In fact, we were changed more than the mountain.   Moreover, those of us who arrived at the mountaintop alive saw what generations of African American mountain climbers before us have seen as they attempted to scale the heights of America's oppressive power: another mountain; there is always another mountain.

After this sobering peek at reality dissolved the romantic visions that had fueled our climb, we came down slowly. We were shaken by what we had seen. We left friends, comrades, dreams, and ideals broken and too often unburied in the crags and crevices of that mountain that was contemporary America. Back in the valley, we did not look forward to the next climb, nor to climbing any more for the rest of our lives. Yet, we did not find the valley hospitable. No rest in the valley. No strength to climb.

Tombstones in the valley and weather-beaten skeletons on the mountain's face mocked whatever plans for any future climbs that we halfheartedly made. Nevertheless, for some of us, there was no other choice. We had to go on, but going on would no longer be joyful.   Sometimes, our very grimness alienate those who would have helped us, who would have joined us. But what were we to do? We could not fake mirth; down to the marrow of our bones we were sad. Young soldiers may look forward to the challenges of war, but old soldiers prefer the search for peace even as they heft their weapons and head out on another mission. Seeing death close up makes one wish for the death of death. But alas, death is the only aspect of life that never dies.

In looking back over the ground I had covered in four decades, the first death that shook me personally was my grandfather on my mother's side. He was a Baptist preacher whose nickname in another life had been "Dude" in deference to his dapper charm. The nickname was so appropriate that even after he had been pastoring two churches it was not unusual to hear someone refer to him as "Dude Copelin," just as if Dude was his given Christian name.

Reverend Copelin smoked cigars, wrote out his sermons, read a great deal, and was active in the Republican Party. I emulated him so much that when I was in junior high school and Nixon and Kennedy ran against each other, I thought Nixon was a better choice, not because of his personality, but because the platform of the Republican Party seemed to make more sense to me. By the time my grandfather died, I had moved to a state of total contempt for the "poli-tricks" of voting. "If voting made a real difference, they'd make it illegal," I contended. Freshly back from the army in 1968, I remember entering a voting booth and not voting for any candidate. All I did was pull a few levers in support of extending benefits for Louisianans who were veterans.

By 1969, we were wrapped up in a serious student struggle at SUNO (Southern University in New Orleans). The situation had become so serious that the national guard was sent in by helicopter to put down the rebellion. Nearly the entire New Orleans police department (without exaggeration) were out to stop us from lowering the American flag and raising the red, black, and green liberation flag. Despite their presence, we raised the liberation flag and took over the school. The battle was on.

Many of us were Vietnam-era armed forces veterans. We were armed with shotguns and carbines. There was nothing Christian-like in our demeanor, our speech, or our intentions.

We wanted revolution, NOW! In an effort to regain control, the SUNO administration called a mass meeting one night with the parents of all the students. My grandfather was there. Many of us sat in the back of the auditorium and guffawed loudly at what we perceived as the inept and transparent lies of the administration. The air was thick with confrontation. We were too cocksure and self-centered to be afraid. We had been in the army. We were young. The whole potential nation of African Americans was rising up, and we were moving on up with it.

Looking back, it is easy to see that I had been groomed to be a preacher. Almost as soon as I had learned to read and speak, I was put in front of audiences. The church taught me to speak to people. And in the movement, I was often on the stump preaching fire and brimstone, raising a fist instead of the Bible, eliciting "right-ons" instead of "amens." But on that night, I do not remember speaking. My grandfather was there and he spoke with incredible passion. Although he wanted to avoid violence, of course (from him that was to be expected), he did not simply side with the administration's tacky solution of pretending that it was a misunderstanding. My grandfather knew, we knew, our parents knew, and even the administration knew, that something was awfully wrong at that school, something like spoiled tuna sandwiches at a picnic. We could not swallow what was being offered as nourishment for our minds.

I remember just listening.

At one point, as I leaned forward out of the slouching, laid-back position I had adopted, my grandfather seemed to be fighting for words. Next, he was down on the floor. I rushed down the sloping seating area of the lecture hall. He was on the floor and people were around him. Something was seriously wrong. My partner Renaldo and I ran to a doctor's house that was only two or three blocks away. (My younger brother was dating this doctor's daughter.) We got to the house in short order, rang the bell, pounded on the door. Finally the doctor came to the door.

He could do nothing. He advised us to call an ambulance. He did not call. He did not offer us the use of his phone. He would not come down the block to see my grandfather. He closed his door. I cursed him. We ran back. My grandfather died four or five hours later. The family looked at me. I looked at me.

I knew that whether I stopped or continued, the struggle would continue—it always continues. The struggle continues partly because these bastards will not stop exploiting us. As fast as one oppressor is laid low, someone else eagerly straps on jackboots and plants a foot on a weaker person's neck. But, I knew, and this knowledge drove me like a fish instinctively swimming upstream against the current, that the main reason *a luta continua** is because some of us will always resist, and I wanted to be one of that "some" who continue to struggle.

Yet, I am no romantic. Even though the struggle always continues, I am aware that we do not always personally continue in the struggle. The image of fighting on after the death of a close friend is common in movies, but it is not a given in real life. In reality, doubts and despair assail you like graffiti on a freshly painted urban wall. I had caused my grandfather's death. Was this student struggle worth my grandfather's death?

My grandfather's collapse was the first time death grabbed me by the throat. I continued in the movement, but a lot of my

---

* "the struggle continues"

formerly cavalier attitudes about death were muted after that. I tried to think a lot more about people's lives and not just the ideals of our movement.

During the height of the SUNO boycott, when we were demonstrating daily, we took time out to go en masse to the funeral of Jean Kelly's mother. Jean had stood sentry by the flag pole all day the first day we took down the American flag and raised the red, black, and green liberation flag. She was not considered one of the leaders, nor one of the tacticians, but I knew it was important that we attend. A couple of hundred students stood quietly outside the church at the funeral's end. It was important to stand, not just when the bullets were firing, but also afterwards, when the dead were buried.

* * * * * * * * * *

Television is urbanizing all of America. We all now live in cities populated by millions and millions of the "same" people, people with the same speech patterns, role models, clothing, food, cars, desires, and social conditions. Millions of people strive to be the same as what they see at seven, eight, nine, and ten p.m. every weekday evening.

Like nearly everyone else in mega-urban America, we crave the same hip new drinks. Currently popular are these "new" wines and soft drinks, both with small amounts of "real" fruit juices added: fantasy laced with reality. We ingest 99-cent, sale-priced, generic fast foods manufactured from chemically inflated poultry and cattle, sold to us by videos of well-fed actors who whistle, sing, joke, and dance, while they eat.

This is a weird urbanization unlike any past development in history because it is an urbanization of the mind regardless of one's physical location. Today, most of us know the fictional and fictionalizing personas of the major networks and mass entertainment media (video, cinema, and cable television) more intimately than we do our neighbors and co-workers. Not only are most of our role models media creations, but, indeed, nobody cares to know a real person who does not don the mask (the clothing, attitude, slang, mannerism) of a non-real media persona.

We are ignoring life in favor of fiction. Hence, life has become less important than imitating fantasy. We do not want to live, we want to fantasize. This desire to live fantasies is a silver stake in the heart of reality. Like the average person running the hurdles against Edwin Moses, reality is too slow to match fantasy. Indeed it is too heavy to lift its legs across all the hurdles one faces in the 90s. Moreover, now that fantasy has been commodified and you can buy the accoutrements of fantasy to cover your real life, why be real? What is there to gain but pain and second place behind a day-glo-colored, hip persona acquired in a "quasi-hermetically" sealed shopping mall? However, there is still death outside, and we still do not know what to do with it. The first death is the physical death of family and friends close to us. Second, there is the death of reality killed by fantasy, the replacement of real people influencing our lives by the influence of media-created personas. And finally, there is the "thanatos" syndrome, the love of death, which afflicts this "throw-away" society.

The Greek-named thanatos syndrome, an instinctual desire for death, seems to power the so-called free enterprise system's drive for profits: death creates more markets. The shorter the life of a commodity, the sooner a replacement has to be bought. The underside of this literally shortsighted vision is that even the essentials of life support (water, air, land, and sunlight) become a commodity. Quality in each of them is now sold at a premium.

Increasingly in urban America (which is where over 75% of the African American population lives) you cannot even buy clean living space because of environmental pollution wrought by profit-motivated, indiscriminate industrialization. Who can escape acid rain and the synthetic chemicals that shape, color, texturize, flavorize, and in some cases permeate, our food supply?

For a long time, environmentalists were pictured as culturally repugnant "fanatics." Because of the way we were led to believe such people talked, dressed, thought, ate creepy-crawly food, and reeked of "egg-headed" unhipness, nobody wanted to be like that. In essence, environmentalists were painted as rich, White, pain-in-the-ass types who had nothing better to do than complain about the lack of trees, and, who had the money to buy meat of naturally raised livestock that cost three times more than "regular" meat in a "regular" supermarket. Most of us could not envision ourselves being that way, nor could we afford it. Convinced that "healthy" living cost too much, we opted for "fast foods for fast times," as one major hamburger chain sloganizes. Actually, we did not "opt," because in general we were not given a real choice. We were socialized to accept the convenience of the synthetic, a "convenience" manufactured to sell commodities strictly for profit.

Therein lies the essence of the thanatos-inspired modern American marketplace. No longer does a manufacturer need to sell marked-up (cost of manufacturing plus profit) commodities which fulfill a physical or social need. Now, a manufacturer can create a desire, manufacture a product to fulfill that artificially created desire, and then sell that product for a significant profit. The modern American food industry, for example, does not exist to feed this nation; it exists mainly to make a profit, and hence will sell as food items that are not food and that have very little, if any, nutritional value.

This scenario is all based on our being blinded by the hi-tech light show. We think that the shadows thrown on the screens of our mind are both a greater and more desirable "reality" than what is happening in the sunlight/moonlight. While it is true that we may "desire" fantasy more than reality, it is one thing to fantasize and another to think that fantasy is reality.

In one of his most sane moments, Huey Newton, comparing the difficulties of revolution in America versus the difficulties the Mao-led Chinese had in making revolution, made the following comment: "Yeah, but Mao didn't have to deal with Mickey-Mouse minds!" A blank page is much easier to deal with than a cartoon-covered mind.

Amusing Ourselves to Death by Neil Postman is an extremely insightful reflection on our current fascination with media-induced fantasy. Yet, most of us will never read Postman's book because most of us no longer read. So used to being cooled-out by the televised image, we "watch" but we do not see, even though we "think" we see.

We watch make-believe and do not bother attempting the difficult task of discerning whether what we are watching is a reflection of reality or a projected fantasy. Moreover, as Postman cogently points out, the medium of television dictates that anything on major network television must, above all else, be entertaining if anyone is to watch it. When reality is repackaged so that it is as entertaining as a sitcom, inevitably our ability and desire to identify reality, not to mention identify "with" reality, is significantly diminished.

We used to talk about right and wrong. Today, there is another layer to deal with: real and unreal. During the 60s, we operated from the dictum that the prevalent reality was wrong and, thus, we had to change it. By the 80s, however, most of us had swallowed the Huxley-predicted Quaalude.* Instead of trying to change our reality (social revolution being the ultimate change), most of us have opted to accept changing ourselves, changing not just what we think, but indeed changing how we think—if, indeed, we think at all.

As hard as it is for many people to accept, reality is more important than our individual opinions or fantasies about reality. Even though most of our actions are guided more by what we have been led to believe or "feel" than by any critical assessment of our own concerning what is actually happening at any given moment, the fact remains that reality is more important than fantasy. Reality is more important, but unfortunately, in most cases, fantasy, false reflections, and assumed beliefs dominate the American mindscape. And what a bizarre mindscape this territory inside our heads has become.

But even this bizarreness goes out the door when the death wagon comes. Whether trying to shape or escape reality, "death don't have no mercy!" We cannot hide from death. Whether we are fantasizing or facing reality, death is there and it is always going to get us.

In the darkness of meditations like that, sooner or later a depressing thought slips upon you and nearly smothers you,

---

* *Brave New World* was a far more accurate predictor of the "Western world" than Orwell's *1984*, although *1984* does apply to the social conditions in too many so-called socialist countries.

choking off the oxygen of hope. I remember feeling my face with my hand, rubbing my body, investigating myself. And the question swooped through the window like a worrisome fly entering through a rip in the screen. It buzzed in the dark. I could not see it; could only hear its annoying noise. There before me was the question, filthy as a fly that has recently fed on horseshit: So, what's the point?

What's the point of anything, of everything? What difference does it make if one struggles? Death is going to claim you, whether you did well or failed miserably. Many people wrestle with that question. Death makes you think. Even if you have never thought serious thoughts for more than five straight minutes in your entire life-time, when death strikes, you start thinking.

This is why America hides death from us, trivializes and deflects death into entertainment. What if we daily were forced to face the victims of America: the hungry and homeless people not viewed on our televisions but camped outside our doors; the beggars and super-exploited laborers of Haiti who manufacture baseballs sitting mutely outside the stadium and brought to us at commercial breaks? What if we had to live encrusted in filth on top of Old Smokey in the Philippines, where popular Vietnam movies are shot? What if we had to languish on Native American reservations with uranium dust eating our lungs out, speaking only in pieces of language because there are no schools to teach us our native tongue or even the language of our conquerors? What if it was our little sister whom we vainly tried to rock to sleep, her tiny voice hoarse from hollering in baby pain because she was born a junkie? If we had to live with real death, the death that happens every day, instead of the amusing death on the screens, then we would do something.

Popular culture has been extremely successful at inspiring us not to recognize death's shadow crossing our own bodies. Like physicians adept at diagnosing disease in others, but blind when it comes to recognizing symptoms of illness in themselves, we find it difficult to recognize that the lives we are living are killing not only others far away who speak a different language, wear a different color skin, or work for U.S.-based corporations in foreign countries for one-fifth the wages we make. It is not just strangers who are the victims. The lives we are living are also killing us.

And we fail to face what is going on because recognition of this reality is psychologically overwhelming. That fly is a monster. It fills the room inside our heads with a buzzing din. After all our own, as well as worldwide, efforts at revolution have seemed to fail to make a major difference, we begin inching toward despair. We are dying, but the fly is still alive. The only way to deal with it, or so it seems, is not to think about it. Not to think about life. Not to think.

During the summer of '86, I did a lot of thinking. But I never killed that fly. I wonder, what is it going to take for us to kill that fly, to take a real look at life?

Many people, lives, relationships, and organizations I loved are gone, but it was their living that taught me invaluable lessons about life. I specifically can remember invaluable lessons that my father taught me, and I strive today to carry forward his teaching. He would always say: "You don't get no credit for what you do for yourself; you suppose to do that. You get credit for what you do for other people."

What is life? Life is a chance—not a certainty, just a chance—to do some good for others, to create some beauty out of what is at hand. Death is a certainty, life is a chance. How

fat or how slim our chances are, that is left to luck and
circumstance. What we do with our chance, that is up to us.

THE MEANING OF LIFE

sometimes I sit
  and I wonder
  what is the meaning
  of life
I sit
sometimes
and I wonder
  and then I realize
  I am the meaning
  of my own life
the meaning is me

Sun Song III

another year w/out
(from a letter to veda)

this has been another year

w/out peace

the insanity of world governments
hurts the dirt
pierces holes in the sky
allows profit to turn sweet rain
into acid
everywhere children lay with legs blown off by land mines
      or their young skulls cracked open by self-administered
      drugs society allows to be cheaply available, or
      small stomachs filled with emptiness, adolescent minds
      perverted by old ideologues trying to prolong
      human stupidity, pre-teen human beings willfully
      misled by cruel adult ignorant
      pretenses that santa claus exists while
      denying the reality of worldwide
      war

this has been another year

w/out peace

i am waiting for tomorrow,
not just another day, another year,
but tomorrow, a truly
different time,
i can concentrate on nothing else for too long
my sixteen-year-old son said matter-of-factly
     talking with me one day about his future,
       "that is, if they
       don't drop the bomb first"

i have seen war
i have seen the rubble left behind
after an economic blitzkrieg levels human labor
into beggars, thieves, prostitutes and aspirant
pop stars who sing in the foreign
language of english / i have photographed
people literally living in mud and worse
been forced by reality to recognize
that their muddy existence
was more prudent than defenselessly
facing remington bullets and
machetes in the night / i hurt
in haiti, sleepless through long nights
constantly hearing the silent
dreadful scream of peasant realities, my
lips moved trembling as i sight-read
jamaica's rhythmic inscriptions
of blood, scrawled screaming
off walls and sidewalks:
"the po / cant take / no mo"

this "another year" is so redundant

i view myself as a political animal
i see juntas to the left, juntas to the right
i am beginning to hate governments
i refuse to tell anyone what to do
i want to shout to everyone i meet
"execute the policeman in your head"
but i am no fool, petty
criminals are the cockroaches
of capitalism, they will callously crawl
into your nose if you sleep too soundly
and eat out your eyeballs from the inside,
i remember right-wing bumper stickers:
"next time your house is robbed, call a hippie,"
so i do not call for anarchy even as
i wish legalities were outlawed, i used to
have a 30-caliber
carbine, i used to believe
in guns even though
i never shot anyone,
arm yrself or harm yrself, like
that, and recently my rifle was
stolen when my father's
house was robbed, i was strong enough
not to replace it,
i am not afraid
i am not afraid to arm myself if necessary
i am not afraid to live unarmed, i am not
afraid, snake-like i am shedding old
ideas which served me well to this point
but i am growing and there is new skin, new
thoughts, deeper stuff
which in its tender growth
was protected by the old, so

my molting is a ritual of regeneration,
not a rejection, i do not denounce
the old skin which sheltered me
i strip reverently and fold
the old cloth gently, i believe
more than ever in the necessity
of revolution, but
one can not strike a
match in a wind storm and expect
to light
a fire

there is so much to think about
and in the midst of another year w/out peace,
the turmoil of unexpected deadends mocking
my every expert navigation
down my life path, yaknow
how we think we are on the highway cruising
in the sun when really we be running
up an alley at night without lights,
we come to the wall and must stop before
we crash and back slowly out, and now
we are hesitant to take any road not known, when
the ship goes astray the captain
cannot blame bad maps, something
must be done, the way ahead must
be found, how do we sail out of the land
locked lake of this, another year

i have been struggling
with my persona, struggling with how to
relate, after personal disasters
i hesitate to inflict myself
on anyone, inflict my bullshit on anyone

anymore, perhaps it is a fear of failure
a fear fed by my recent ...(some words
are too painful to say twice in so short
a space), sometimes i look up into
a mirror as i splash water on my hands
after urinating or in the morning
brushing my teeth, or see me walking thru
the hallway on the way out the house, i
see myself in the mirror behind the phone
and wonder why
or how or when or if ever i should
love again

this has been another one of those years
w/out peace

right now i am waiting
for tomorrow,
it is monday night,
i have been reading world
literature, the guardian, in
these times, *and listening to betty*
carter, sade and al green, composing
this letter/poem, and talking to
a young mother
on the phone who has three
kids and is molding herself
into a sensitive photographer and
committed writer / and
i'm wondering,
wondering what
will i say or do to create
a real
tomorrow,

i wish the uncertainty was over
do we want to go through another
year w/out world peace, another year
of personal turmoil

it is so easy to be alone
it is so hard to be alone
don't call anyone, don't chance anything
go to work, go home, go somewhere,
don't go anywhere
read, drink, movies, records, parties
where we show our teeth, an occasional
kiss, a moment (now almost just a memory) here
or there of sexual activity, on television a black
man leaves south africa forever, he says
exile is like dying, we are in exile
from real life, this living is like dying,
in the daily papers the headlines are
about football teams and not the senseless
murdering of people found floating in
the lake, face down in empty lots, on
sidewalks, the backs of their
heads blown away, i've got to get out
of this year, get out of all years like this
w/out peace

i want to be optimistic about the ability
of human beings to love each other
but i am barely a survivor
i came through with nothing
but the clothes on my back, the ideas
in my head, last i remember, optimism was
right behind me, when i made

the corner and peeped
back around, there was nothing
there but another year,
huffing and puffing, another
year, bent over, hands on its
knees, out of breath, tongue hanging
out, not able to go much further, at
the end of its chain of days, december, another
year, i look closer and see the material
of my shirt's back torn at the beast's feet,
i want to be optimistic about the ability
of human beings to love, but the natural
inclination is to protect one's back, to cover
one's heart and believe only
in the abstract
about the alleged ability
of humans to love

but enough belly aching
let's make music
let's dance,
let us, each of us, all of us
be honest with each
other, hang soft
make and greet a new
year together, whatever,
something, i swear i
don't want to see another
year w/out

peace!

let's dance

let's dance to the music
of a new year
even as we create it

let's dance
and create, and struggle
and love so that there will
never again
be another year
w/out

On Loneliness & Alienation

Even for Siamese twins, all of us are alone. All of the social rituals of bonding—from informal gangs of friends as children to professional associations as adults, from puppy love to life-long dedication to major causes, from traditional hetero-sexual marriage to male or female bonding—are designed to mitigate the distress of loneliness and alienation that every human being encounters at one time or another. African Americans not only encounter loneliness and alienation, we are encased in both all of our lives. Both permeate the food we eat, the air we breath, and every song we sing in this strange land.

I think about both loneliness and alienation, as they affect me as an individual as well as how they affect me as just one of many African Americans struggling with days and nights in the United States. This is my brooding, especially when I experi-ence and remember the nights alone (especially when someone else slept next to me), and I hear Louis Armstrong singing with a heart-rending seriousness, "Lord, you made the night too long."

Few of us talk about loneliness and alienation directly, and probably fewer of us even think about it at all—except to feel blue when a relationship is in crisis or does not work out, when the job gets to us, or we lose our job, or on other similar occasions. When these occasions hit, rather than get philosophical, we usually join the chorus and sing along with Louis Armstrong, not the sophisticated moan of "Lord, you made the night too long," but the more famous existential cry, "What did I do to be so Black and blue?"

ALIENATION AND THE SENSE OF SELF

In reflecting on the question of loneliness and alienation, I must first consider my own social state. As of 1986, I am separated from a 16-year marriage. Only recently have I begun to deeply relate to my children beyond the contact that passes for normal parenting in modern America; yes, I drove the kids to school and stuff like that, but it is now, as they move into the world on their own, that we become much closer. I know this is my struggle, not theirs.

I am sure that my children have always wanted to be close to me. They have expressed this desire as well as their exasperation about my absence in various ways. Yet it is only now that three of them are living on their own that I have been able to move beyond the generality of being a parent/guardian and actualize the intimacy of close friendship. Tayari, their mother, has been much more successful at building this type of friendship, which I personally never missed, but which I deeply value as I begin to build it. Rather than couch this friendship in some vague pop-psychological terms about the inability of men to express their feelings, I examine myself. From there, I am able to move inward. I look at myself as a man (subject to all the forces which shape and unshape manhood in general and Black manhood specifically) and as a human product of America.

For African Americans, a category of human existence which is by nature contradictory (Black in White America, marginal to the mainstream, the descendants of enslaved

Africans in a country that has always been synonymous with freedom for White males), we contain and grow within ourselves the seeds of self-destruction. This self-destructive growth is a direct result of a socially induced psychosis and a destructive nurturing by the dominant society. Although we did not willfully sow these seeds, most of us unfortunately, reap the debilitating results in one tragic form or another.

For us, life is a concoction that epitomizes the concepts of sweet-and-sour contained in one sauce. Moreover, for us, life is more than just a struggle to taste all the sweetness we can without choking on the inevitable surfeit of sourness. Life is also a struggle to make cosmic sense out of this throw of the dice of our existence upside the wall of 20th-century America. So, we are searching for sweet and valiantly trying not to gag on sour, but we are also trying to resolve the great questions: What am I here for? Why was I born? And, of course, the all-time number one hit among our people: What did I do to be so Black and blue?

The curse of Ham does not begin to explain these last 500 years in the wilderness of the Western hemisphere. As profound as they are within the context of life as they knew and lived it, none of the intellectual achievements of Euro-centric philosophers—from Hegel to Sartre, from Rousseau to B. F. Skinner, from Calvin to Primo Levi*—explains our existence. Only Primo Levi even comes close to aptly describing the abyss we regularly and painfully tiptoe across (balancing ourselves with the stick of African humanism), inching our way along the tightrope of an existence well-greased by the pathologies of colonialism. None of these major Western philosophers begins

---

* a Jewish death camp survivor who tragically committed suicide many years after WWII.

to approach the profoundness it takes to live life daily as a descendant of enslaved Africans, a struggle that insists we run through the maze of modern America, while caught up in a rat race we perpetually lose.   Indeed, African Americans are caught up in a race toward a distant goal that has never been concretely identified. Yet, this goal is continuously mythologized in the dream state (as in "I have a dream").

We hurl ourselves toward a prize that at best may be a trinket of dubious value. Once we approach and/or acquire this trinket, we may realize that we really do not want it. It may be a prize we actually despise. Worse yet, seizing this prize may pull the switch on our own electrocution. For us to succeed in America requires that we kill ourselves, figuratively (cultural suicide) and literally (the uplift of a few at the expense of the majority).

These are the kinds of questions I contemplate in regard to loneliness and alienation. I am not approaching this stuff on an abstract level. I am thinking more specifically about my life in the body&soul sense: what I have been going through, what I know some of my friends are going through, and what will also be helpful to others grappling with this same, ubiquitous, double-headed monster pounding at my/our door.

Alienation is a major part of our essential problem. Alienation, the separation of labor from product, responsibility from deeds, part from the whole, is essentially the best definition one can offer about our relationship as a people to America. Our alienation is a separation made more painful by our proximity to the powers that enforce our alienation as well as the realities and dreams from which we are alienated. I can see America, I can hear America, smell it every morning, but the price of holding America close is alienation from my people. Initially, it is simply a matter of class alienation, but then it goes deeper.

Stage one: the old "I'm your color but not your kind" alienation. At first we simply talk better, dress less wildly, and eat in restaurants where at least two forks are set on the table. Next, we move out of the 'hood and into a planned community. Yet, all of that is nothing compared to what happens as we get closer to making it in America, whether as a banker, entertainer, lawyer, or drug dealer.

Stage two: here we are invariably sucked into a vortex of alienation. The more we advance in our chosen profession, the further away we move from the masses of our people. This distancing is the same for all professionals of whatever ethnicity. However, when African American professionals arrive at our new social station, more likely than not we are either the only or one of only a handful of African Americans living and working at that level. There is no dominant community of successful African American professionals; the community of successful professionals is overwhelmingly White or corporate/academic-oriented.

All those "national associations" of Black this and that professionals that were created during segregation, as well as those ethnic and women's caucuses founded in the 70s and 80s are generally adjuncts to the established order. These organizations are little more than psychological self-help groupings where members commiserate with each other about the frustrations and futilities of their jobs. These associations serve an important function in raising self-esteem among their members, but few of them definitively impact their professions beyond providing opportunities for networking for a better job. Today, the majority of Black professional organizations are financially (and sometimes psychologically) dependent on the mainstream for their existence. For example, Black doctors who would seem to be the most independent are actually financially and structurally dependent on the mainstream for medicines, tools, facilities, etc., and psychologically incapable of operating solely or mainly within the Black community. This state of increased dependency despite ascendancydency of the professional ranks leads to the third level.

Stage three: the deepest alienation is the alienation of our essential self from our public persona. We all have to deal with this reality. We walk around daily hoisting an incredibly heavy public persona, but in our most intimate moments we face the fact—regardless of how many degrees or titles, regardless of how much money we make— that each of us is struggling with an uncertain future and our possessions do nothing to mitigate the depression that results from that fact.

Perhaps, one of the saddest examples of this phenomenon is the failure of the children of professional Blacks to build on their parents' accomplishments. It is almost axiomatic to read about the son or daughter of a famous Black personality having personal or criminal problems. While some may think this is an isolated phenomenon, we are losing far more young people than is generally imagined.

What do we really gain once we achieve the American Dream? On the one hand, I am an American citizen. I live and work in New Orleans. On the other hand, I am very different from the norm, very different. However, the alienation that I choose—self-determined separation—is different from the alien-ation that is enforced by outside powers, often against my will and without any regard to what may or may not be good for me or my people. The real deal is this: no matter how much any of us might try to fit in, all of us are subject to those unchosen forces of alienation that are euphemistically referred to simply as "the powers that be."

At one point, this was going to be an essay on sex, some of my observations and thinking about it vis-a-vis a major preoccupation of many of our people. I soon realized that sex was only one manifestation of the larger concern. Although sex is an interesting topic, the sex issue alone does not really capture the essence of why our existence is so precarious, so troubling, and so goddamn hard to handle.

On a recent album by the reunited group *The Time,* there is this brilliantly illustrative moment when Morris Day calls out for some "horns." He wants to hear some horns. What kind of horns do we hear? A chorus of synthesizers imitating horns. The truly tragic aspect of this illustration is not that Day would dare foist off synthesizers as horns, but rather, that most listeners don't catch it and really do not care even after it is pointed out to them. Who cares whether Morris Day dances to real horns? Who cares that many pop stars are lip-syncing rather than singing at live concerts? I use the example of music because music is the language of our "inner nation," and when our music becomes synthesized and lip-synced, what does that say about our souls?

After the 80s, the Decade of Conformity, what we are left with is the same dull, albeit deadly, position we have always been in: between a rock and a hard place, except maybe now the rock is made of steel and the hard places where we reside are physically more dangerous and socially more desolate than ever. This is the alienation that does the most harm because the separation of our lives in the present from any hope of a brighter tomorrow, precisely marks off the breeding ground of existential despair. When people no longer have anything to value, then literally everything is, or quickly becomes, expendable. What we are witnessing is the alienation of the self from the future. The nihilism of the ghetto is no accident but rather the logical conclusion of America's genocidal policy of social control of African Americans.

Of course we do not all physically live in the ghetto, but mentally, the music group *War* was right, "the world is a ghetto," and the ghetto is a killing ground. The alarmingly high rate of homicide in this nation's inner cities is nothing but environmentally induced social suicide.

COMMUNITY

The grimness of our current conditions starkly indicates our need for wholeness, communication, connection, and community. Where we went wrong was in seeking and/or accepting integration when what we really needed was wholeness as a self-reliant and self-determined people. An instinctual recognition of this distinction was evident in our embracing the call for Black Power, an objective which was abandoned as we went deeper into trying to make change by working within the system. Our trip into integration resulted in a deeper futility which actually heightened our alienation and fragmented our meager resources.

After the 80s, where are our cultural institutions, businesses, schools, religious institutions, and political organizations? All integration did for us was obdurate the negative effects of alienation and scattered what thin human and material resources we had to the wiles and whims of corporate America.

On an individual level, the most frequent manifestation of alienation is loneliness. To escape loneliness in modern America, one must struggle to build community. Given today's lifestyle, building any kind of community is indeed a fierce struggle. Community is no longer a birthright. We are no longer born into a nourishing nexus of grandparents, aunts, uncles, and multi-generational, non-biologically related adults who actually function and are accepted by us as parents. Additionally, we no longer experience care and support from a plethora of adults as we move through school and into the world of work.

Today, we are usually birthed by a mother who valiantly struggles to raise us with or without the assistance of our father. If one grows up without community, it is difficult and almost impossible to create community as an adult because one does not know what community really is.   And never having experienced it or been systematically taught what community is, one is incapable of the emotionally taxing work that building community requires. Building community is neither easy nor a given simply because we might want to do so. In many ways, for our people in the 90s, building community is like overturning a boatload of non-swimmers in the middle of a stormy lake miles away from shore. Very few, if any, of them will make it to shore alive. Not because they are incapable of learning how to swim, but rather because tossed about in the middle of raging waters without instruction and practice is absolutely the worst and most difficult way to learn to swim.

The boat is going down. How many of us really know how to swim? No matter how desperately we may want to reach the shore, the fact is that if we do not know how to swim, our chances are slim—very, very slim. Our ancestors who survived slavery came from societies that consciously and systematically prepared them to function as a community of adults. What instructions have we had?

RELATIONSHIPS

I both feel and know this inability to construct community on the most personal of levels. As a man living his fifth decade alone and without a "significant other," on one level my aloneness is a choice. But on another level it is also a result of my own failure. I know that the reality of much of my self-made decision is actually deeply circumscribed by the weight and effects of my failure in marriage. Whether we recognize it or not, after such failure, most of us vow never again to subordinate ourselves in a relationship, never again to submerge our individual needs and desires to such an extent that we do anything or put up with anything in order to keep the marriage going. With those kinds of attitudes directing us to circle our emotional wagons around our wounded egos, is it any wonder that many of us become, if not out-and-out cynical, at least extremely wary of entering into future relationships? Many, many people are asking the question: can African American men and women live together? Obviously we can. Some of us are doing so now, and many of us have done so in the past. Nevertheless, the answer is more often, "No, I cannot."

This alienation we are experiencing between women and men seems to be deeper than the alleged eternal battle between the sexes. Is this really a question concerning the nature of relationships between individuals in today's modern society who enter into legal and personal partnerships that generally include sexual intimacy? This same question could be asked about homosexual couples. Although the problem is usually framed in the context of a battle of the sexes, it's really deeper than that. Witness all the struggles women face who are working to build community among themselves. They may think that much of their problems are the result of the negative effects of being reared in and affected by a sexist society, but a significant part of what they experience is the alienation of individuals from society/community. The problem, then, is not really about the inability of the sexes to get along. Society-wide, we are running into the forces of alienation at work in modern America, forces that push each of us away from uniting with others and toward atomization.

Atomization is the starkest form of the much ballyhooed "rugged American individualism." We will not overcome it unless we begin now to deal with understanding how the major social forces work on individuals, especially those forces that are corporate controlled and directed. The political, economic, and social forces, such as the mass media and entertainment complexes, are often more dominant than the nuclear family and the church. Unless we recognize how these forces have shaped (twisted) each of us and work at countering them, how can we hope to develop strong relationships?

Moreover, there is still another gap to bridge. For most of us, whether we admit it or not, sex is one of the major issues we must face—not just the nature of sexual exchanges between partners in a relationship, but also sexual behavior outside of the relationship (monogamous or non-monogamous). Within the Catholic church, the question of celibacy and the sexual (mis)conduct of priests has become a major issue. AIDS-related questions of safe sex, the proliferation of video pornography, and prostitution, all point to an incredible and more pervasive societal emphasis on sexual activity that is greater now than in previous identifiable eras.

I am not saying that these issues were never on the table before, nor that people did not engage in a variety of sexual activity before. Yet, sex has a higher priority, as far as personal activity goes, than it has ever had in the history of America. This is partially a result of our being sociologically conditioned to elevate the quantity and quality of sexual activity to a mythological status of fantasy and desire.

We have also been conditioned to engage in a broader variety of sexual conduct than in the past. One community resident in New Orleans noted, in typically salty fashion, that all we got out of integration was "going with White women and eating pussy." Crude as that description may be, the general acceptance of oral sex as normal sexual activity (even by those who don't like the practice or who would prefer not to engage in the activity) is one indication of both the effectiveness and pervasiveness of the sexual conditioning of our community that has been effected since the 50s.

The end result is not simply a change in our sexual activity and values, but more importantly a change in our priorities. Some say that our society is fixated on sex. Regardless of whether we believe that to be the case, there is no denying that sex plays a major role in today's relationships. While some argue that we are more sexually enlightened and others argue that we are more sexually corrupt, I argue that we are more sexually oriented and we are now clearly more oriented toward making individual decisions about sex than toward accepting traditional or community established norms. These individual decisions are generally triggered and informed by the ubiquitous display of sex in all levels of today's society – especially with regard to the commodification and commercialization of objects based on how obtaining said objects will make one feel.

Isn't it paradoxical that while there is a greater emphasis on individual choice there is a correspondingly greater publicizing of what once was intimate and private behavior? Read a newspaper; check out the advertisements and the description of crimes. Look at television; you'll get the picture. Whether conscious of it or not, we have been conditioned to think that something is wrong with us or something is missing in our lives if we are not sexually active. So what do we do? Well, in the absence of an ideology and/or methodology for problem solving, we do what we have been conditioned to do.

While we may make individual choices and think we are self-driven in our decision making, actually, we are only reflecting the corporate induced tendency toward atomization. Many of us do not recognize that the modes of our thinking, the tendencies we display, often the thoughts we think and the decisions we make have actually been inculcated by sophisticated behavior modification at the macro-social level. Whether we turn left or right, go forward or backward, most of us are still traveling on the road constructed by corporate America, a road that downplays establishing strong self-determined relationships in favor of atomization and submission to the power of corporate-determined social norms.

Rather than find self-worth in participation in community, we now vainly attempt to achieve these goals through individual acquisition and "self-actualization." Unfortunately, many of us do not realize that we are human beings and not machines. Our essential nature is that we are social creatures and not autonomous beings who can achieve full development through watching one's diet, daily exercise, a good job, a fat bank account, and, oh yes, practicing safe sex with whomever we choose. There is no short cut to mental health. As human beings, we need help. We cannot do it alone.

One result of all of this is that it becomes difficult to establish and sustain relationships that do not reinforce atomization or corporate established social norms. The American ruling class, which publicly denies its own existence (all the better for it to function unobserved) even as it concentrates and wields more and more power, encourages us to either join the mainstream as a paid employee or to act only as an individual entrepreneur going for self-aggrandizement. In keeping with this orientation, alternatives to corporate/individual dualism are usually denigrated by the mass media. (For example, nontraditional religions are generally and pejoratively referred to as "cults.")

Faced with the steamroller of corporate might, it does not take the average individual long to see the wisdom of going along with the general scheme of life as we know it. We do not even realize how much of our day-to-day functioning is simply the result of how we have been trained to function. We think we are making up our own minds about an issue or behavior, but are only doing just as we have been trained to do.

In modern America, strong interpersonal relationships are not valued as a number-one priority, regardless of how much some of us say we want a strong relationship. I have seen myself, time and time again, place my personal goals above the goals of a relationship. Although I, like most other people, claim to be about building group efforts, I move about based on what I believe in and what my personal goals are. There are very few of us in general and very few men specifically who can honestly prove by our deeds that a relationship, a marriage, for example, is more important than our personal goals. In fact, many of us secretly question the validity of the old icons of American society, especially the nuclear family and the institution of marriage.

A significant number of people, especially women, are no

longer willing to put up with marriage as it is traditionally defined—ditto for any number of other social formations, from job commitments to religious affiliations. These traditional formations are often generally criticized as being what the Marxists call bourgeois, what the feminists call sexist, and what people of color recognize as racist. Yet, we are often at a loss to create a new society without definitive social formations. The very act of moving toward liberation from the old often dovetails with the forces of atomization. Our often-justified criticisms of the status quo, and subsequent rejection thereof, leads us to place the maintenance of traditional relationships at a low level.

Having been beset by a myriad of hardships from the larger social structure and by various substructures within the larger society, we find ourselves, often unconsciously, opposing any structure other than those that we personally believe in at the moment. Of course, the inverse often happens. Frustrated by trying to find an alternative, many people lapse into a nostalgia for a presumed "good, old fashioned" approach to our problems. We allow ourselves to fantasize that Christianity, for example, is the solution, or that we need to return to the "traditional" family. We wait and pray for the return of "God." Unable to find a solution under contemporary conditions, we look for a solution outside of the here and now, whether in some future "kingdom" to come or the security of a romanticized past.

Now, more than ever, what we really need is to figure out ways to work together, to learn from and love one another. If organized religion helps one do that, then so be it. However, regardless of the philosophy, it is the deed that counts, and any philosophy that does not teach us to oppose oppression and exploitation as well as build community will not succeed in solving our problems.

Now, more than at any time in the last ten years, I find myself struggling to build community at a multitude of levels. Many of the projects I initiate involve working with others. On the one hand, this is very much a reflection of where I am personally. On the other hand, I am finding more and more people receptive to the concept. Many people are taking on the struggle to build community, a concept that hurdles over the problems of constructing interpersonal, one-on-one relationships and moves to the more inclusive level of work based on shared values or objectives. Building community is a major step forward in reversing the alienation trend so characteristic of the 80s and the alleged wisdom of integrating into the system.

As the aftermath of the 80s attests, the last decade was indeed a time of deep alienation, a time of vain attempts at achieving success through integration and conforming to mainstream (i.e., corporate or marketplace) norms. Successfully forging a symbiotic synthesis of the two generally contradictory aspects of our nature (African and American), while simultaneously excelling within the strictures of the American mainstream, is the loneliest success in the world. From politician and preacher to entertainer and athlete, we have found that walk to be a walk we had to make alone—a walk that took us away from our community. Many who took the road in the 80s are beginning to reject it now. Due to the narrowness of the highway, the heavy tolls every quarter-mile or so, and the rigors of the travel, which required vehicles of qualification far beyond the meager means of the majority of our people, this was a walk that most of us could not afford to take—even when we wanted to.

African Americans' inherent alienation from the mainstream has complicated our struggle to fit in. From acquiring the requisite higher education to climbing the corporate/academic ladder, every step up meant a step away from the Black self and toward the White other. Not surprisingly, many of us failed and those of us who succeeded in conforming and excelling often found ourselves in frustratingly lonely and unhappy surroundings. Generally, however, those most negatively affected were our children.

The failure of many of us to achieve satisfactory success as individuals in the 80s will invariably lead to our inability to rebuild community among our people in the 90s. While some pundits continue to argue for buying into the American mainstream, the hard facts remain that there is little room for us there. Further, the well-being and prosperity of the mainstream is directly contingent upon our continued subjugation. In many, many ways, the overall picture is depressing.

A Jewish businessman who does not live as an orthodox Jew and who therefore is generally perceived by New Orleanians as White, asked me one day during a tete-a-tete which he requested: how could I have hope in the future, in people? Although our conversation meandered, my initial response to this question centers on my understanding that I come from a people who have survived chattel slavery—the most stringent stripping away of humanity ever imaginable—and yet did not lose hope. I come from a people whose history has prepared me to deal with alienation, and though it makes me blue, I retain hope that "the sun's gon shine in my back door someday." I have no rationale for my belief that we as a people can and will overcome the seemingly inevitable self-inflicted annihilation that threatens the existence of humanity as a species and indeed the planet earth as an inhabitable environment. Just as no scientist, sociologist, philosopher, or theologian has offered a reasonable explanation for the Black sense of rhythm, perhaps there is also no explanation for our apparent ability to deal with alienation and consistently strive for community.

THE SOLUTION

As trite or cliched as it may sound, the truth of the matter is that we are lovers. This identity of ours is indelibly encoded into our genes. Love is the only antidote for loneliness and alienation, starting with the self, moving through family, neighborhood, and community touching race, nation, and ultimately the world. Since we were the first humans, we were the first to love. Given the state of the world today, it seems we may be the last to love. Perhaps because we have been living and loving for so long, it is our nature to be lovers. Regardless of the actions of individuals amongst us or of social forces upon us, we are lovers. As insubstantial as it may sound to many people, that is the sum total and irreducible essence of the uniqueness of the Black psyche: we are lovers. And what is love but a searching for synchronization and uplifting of the whole of a situation, a way to simultaneously submerge the differences and raise the shared essentials? The so-called self-effacement of love is never a negation of the self, but rather an expansion of the self (a lesson we have been trying to teach the West for a long time).

For the longest, I resisted understanding that while we work on a long-term solution to our problems as African Americans, each of us as individuals is compelled to solve our own problem of how to find and maintain love. This effort is a major aspect of our overall struggle. Love is the answer, but not in a romantic sense or in a sense that does not recognize differences and the difficulties in dealing with differences. Love is the answer, but not love in the sense of negating the self in an effort to be like the other; rather, love is the answer in the sense that I recognize I am responsible not only for myself and my actions but also for helping others when and where I can. In helping others, I make life better for all—myself included. Because love must start with self, the road to which is often the hardest journey and the awareness of which is the toughest lesson to learn and apply, those who would love others had better first take the advice of our African ancestors: know thyself!

When I listen to our inner-nation language, Black music, I hear love songs, sometimes flowered over in sugary romanticism, sometimes raked through the dirt of blusey cynicism, but love songs nonetheless. Always there, always sung. Listen to our music, the undeniable propensity for love is there.

In any case, the point is that the goal of love is always union, never dissolution; always community, never alienation. Lovers hate separation. We prefer a harmonious whole any day. In all of our self-determined forms of self-expression, from how we eat and dance and make music to how we work and play as teams, all of us are marked by a profound respect for and proclivity toward interaction (i.e. love manifested). Thus exists the prevalence of ritual among us—the providential and salubrious results, feelings, vibes, tingles; the arrived-at psychological, sociological, and even physiological state endemic to successfully constructed community—that tells us, like no words: there is nothing better than love.

Without exception, there is nothing better than love. And this knowledge, this orientation, this religion and/or way of life, makes it possible for us to bear up under the strain of being entrapped in this land where money means more than love to the controllers of this society. In a profound sense, our very lives and loves are proof that America is wrong and our ancestral legacy of love in life is absolutely correct. Were it not for love, Africans in America, as a particular branch of the human species, would be extinct.

Sun Song IV

uncle dewey

as i mature
i wonder
how we made it

we being
the men in my family
the various
african-american males
who colorfully crossed
past bold confusions
intentionally engendered
by the infamous hidden
alabaster hands
of america's human
marketplaces

i meditate on the movements
of these men of color negotiating
the mined maze of making a living
while trying to stay alive

their record setting artful
broken field runs dashing
through pinholes of daylight
flash a fleet form
my flat feet strain to follow

at thirty-three

many whitemen are just hitting
their stride, jauntily jogging
& jolting toward the forty thou
or better mark, the highwater club
& regal scotch, the redwood hot tub
& gold credit card, the CEO position,
the pretty secretary, the sleek
low slung sports car, the trip to Tahiti,
the silk suits, the expensive
business luncheons and tax deductible
donations to the party

at thirty-three

somewhere outside that charmed
circle we black men deftly dance
countering time and disappointments
with loquacious saxophone solos
and other acts of black male
anger/anguish/love&happiness

i am thinking of a man i never really knew
and can only once remember, my uncle dewey,
but it could be either of my deceased
grandfathers who were
both preachers
and one of whom was run out of
Donaldsonville, Louisiana because
he was going to shotgun a white man
long before i acquired a carbine,
he died seeking refuge from a hurricane
in one of his closets as the city "fathers"
sent hurricane Betsy's flood waters
crushing cross our roofs in '65,

the other they called "dude Copelin,"
raised two churches, one in the city, one
in the country and was an active republican,
he died of a stroke which struck
while he forcefully spoke at a rally
called to discuss our student strike and
takeover of the campus where i revolted

it could be either of these men
i am remembering, trying now, as
i get older, to understand and
emulate the spirit chaser/spirit catcher
parts of them, the steel stuff
that survived and did not melt
nor give way under the tempering
of times during which the twisting
of black men happened as regularly
and as routinely as the wringing of
plump chickens' necks on feasting sundays

ten years ago
no one could have told me
i would be thinking about these
old men, old men whom i then
seldom talked to or looked at,
and certainly hoped never
to look like, old men, and
their image, their ideas,
their way of wearing the mask,
of making the mask, of smashing
the mask

i could be thinking about my father
or a lot of people like him
but right now it is my uncle dewey

- i don't even remember how we were
related, all i know is that he lived
next door when i was younger than five, &
wore a dark colored sporting hat
i have no other recollections
of him, not how he looked,
whom he married (was he married?),
how tall he was, what his voice sounded
like or nothing, i only remember calling
him uncle dewey, and this one other
important scene:

he came making it home one day
walking down lizardi street
with an alligator over his shoulder
i tasted alligator meat that evening
cut into little cubes and fried, the
tail tasted sorta like chicken
that's all i remember
just that one unfading image:
walking down our street
past the hedges and the china ball tree
with an alligator on his shoulder

but that's enough, that's a plenty
if only i can embody that black eloquent
strolling through the spaces i move
returning home at dusk
from the workplaces/the social
slaughterhouses with nary a drop of blood
messing up my mean cleanness, no malice
on my mind, and just a grinning wide
with some kind of alligator tossed
casually cross my shoulder

Across Troubled Waters

Black Fathers and Extended Family

I was glad to see 1987—I don't even remember where I was when the new year came in, or what I was doing. I was simply glad that 1986 was over.

On Friday morning, January 30th, I took my father to see a doctor. He said he had not slept well that night. I had been out. Keith (my youngest brother who is a cardiologist) was away at a medical convention in San Francisco. Keith had checked Daddy before leaving and also left the name of a doctor to see should anything go wrong.

We went to the doctor that Keith recommended. He had no answers for my father's discomfort. As a precaution, he decided to admit my father to the hospital for further testing. My father insisted on going back home first. His sister Ida Mae was there along with a friend of my father's from high school, Jerri. They agreed to take him to the hospital and I left for work.

When I spoke to my father later that evening, he said he was feeling better. They were running tests, but there was no word. I told him I would come by a little later. He said he was fine and wanted to rest because he had not slept the night before. He did not want visitors until the next day. Feeling unsure, I went to the hospital anyway.

My father was walking around when we got there. There still were no results on the tests. He assured me that he felt better and that everything was going to be all right. After we visited awhile, he told me he would see me in the morning. That was the last time we talked. On Friday night, he went into a coma. He never regained consciousness.

Keith, Kenneth (my middle brother), and I were all present when my father died. There was nothing memorable or even emotionally shattering about my father's death. No last-minute vigorous resistance, no one shouting "no" or throwing themselves across the bed. He just stopped breathing. And that was it. Or so I thought. As time would tell, his death that silent Sunday afternoon was not "it."

I walked around dazed. I had been prepared for my mother's death, but I was totally unprepared for my father's death. Before he died, I believed that I was closer to my mother. But after my father died, I was made to know in ways that I never realized before that Daddy was a sure thing in a world of maybes, probables, hoped-fors, and failures.

I remember when Hoyt Fuller died, the pain I felt but managed to keep at a distance. Then there was the time when I read of Eric Dolphy's death many months after he passed. I was home on leave from the army and was standing in the main New Orleans public library reading back issues of *Downbeat*. There it was. I was shocked. Hurt. I wrote a poem that was angry and bitter. It expressed the rage I felt. I believed that Eric Dolphy was both too young and too important a musician to just "die." Coltrane's death did not hit me quite as hard as Eric's, but it also deeply saddened me. On the day I got the news that Hoyt was dead, I also heard that Marley was dead. But none of that was immediate in my life, although Hoyt Fuller was very important to me as a writer. He had helped and encouraged me. He had published and criticized my work. He had been an example. Yet, between me and all these deaths there was a distance, a space within which I could compose myself and feel better or maybe not feel at all, but still a space to work through the grief.

For long periods after my father's death, I felt like I was drowning in waves of emotions and odd sensations. These sensations would wash over me at various, unexpected times. Sometimes family friends would say something like, "We're really gonna miss your father." And I would think: "Miss him, sheeit, you don't know—you can't know what missing is about." For a couple of seconds, I would go blank. I had never crossed this bridge before, and handling it all was confusing.

I was now the oldest of the Ferdinand men. That thought was a big wave. There were so many expectations and assumed responsibilities tied into being the oldest male, expectations and assumed responsibilities that I had been either refuting or not accepting.

I remember when my mother died and the day my youngest brother "disowned" me. At that moment, he wanted a big brother, someone to take charge and care. Somehow neither of us thought of my father doing it all. We were on the front steps of my house on Tennessee Street, and Keith was angry with me. I told him "No, don't put that on me. If you think it ought to be done, then *you* do it." He told me I was not his brother anymore. The repercussions were so deep that I will never forget how Keith reacted, even now, well after we have settled those differences.

I had already moved away from continuing the tradition of the family name when I changed my name in 1970 at a Kwanzaa ceremony. At that time, everything we did was an act of will, our own will against the world. We were young and inexperienced enough to believe, to actually believe, that our will could carry the day, and, if not carry the day, at the very least carry us as far as we felt like going. I never asked my parents permission. I was not living with them at the time, and frankly, never even thought about asking them.

I had chosen "Kalamu ya Salaam" — first because it literally meant "Pen of Peace," which was my greatest ambition: to be a writer whose work contributed to real peace for our people. Second, I chose it because it was a Swahili name, which meant that it was derived from a non-tribal African language used across national boundaries as a trade language. At that time, Swahili was the only African language that was the sole official language of an African country. Most of the African countries had European languages as the official language. So, instead of my son being Vallery Ferdinand, IV, he was named Mtume ya Salaam.

Both my mother and my father called me Kalamu, although it was not uncommon to hear them sometimes say (as did most of their friends) "Li'l Val" or "Val-ry" (which was the way my birth name was usually pronounced). The people who named me accepted me changing the name they gave me.

My change of name was just one very visible example of my break with tradition and my break with my family, a fissure that caused my brother Keith a lot of pain. I guess Keith thought that I did not care, and certainly he rejected my way of caring and moving ahead. In retrospect, I had boxed off a lot of traditional feelings and was flying ungrounded on the wings of youthful visions of Black people overcoming and uprising. A truer, deeper Black consciousness would have found a way to carry tradition with it, but I was young at that time. I did not know deep.

Keith was rightfully reacting to what he correctly perceived to be his brother's denial of the responsibility of being
a "big brother." In my mind, I was not really denying that
responsibility. I believe we all have a responsibility to and for
each other that stretches far beyond the accidents of birth and
outmoded notions of "family" or something equally rational
and equally unrealistic.

With my father's death, suddenly, like it or not, acknowl-
edge it or not, I was the "head" of the family. I realized with
sadness that if continuity and continuance depended on me,
then the Ferdinand family was ended. I would not carry that
tradition on. The Ferdinands, like so many, many other Black
families, would fragment; the nexus of grandparents, uncles,
aunts, cousins, children, mothers and fathers would become
too far flung and too unrelated in day-to-day ways to any longer
be a family in the old sense of the word.

My sadness was not just that the extended Ferdinand
family was gone. My special sadness was that I was not sure how
to call it back together. Moreover, I was not sure that I really
wanted to call that particular family back together. I was sure
of that for a lot of reasons; some I had thought about, some I
had never thought about. Indeed, as far back as I could
remember, on my father's side of our family, the family was
already untogether. The calabash was broken. And worse than
the calabash being broken, I had nothing to replace it with.
Ahidiana was gone. My nuclear family was gone. Households
and individuals remained, but they were loose and individually
rolling stones, rolling pebbles really cause we ain't kicking up
much dust.

At times, after my father's death, I felt alone, even though
I knew I was not alone. Although there were close friends and

relatives caring for me, they were not inside my head when I slept, when I dreamed, when my father's spirit spoke to me. Sometimes, I still feel alone. I am trying to understand the loneliness of Black manhood, especially post-forty Black manhood, when there is no bright future of promise before you, only a past of Black reality that must be assessed, digested, and dealt with.

Today, as a conscious Black man I realize how my father shaped my life. When he left, I discovered how much of him had been there, how much of him gave form to who I was and who I would become. My ultimate end is not clear to me, but my direction has been well defined by my father's passing through this world and, indeed, sometimes his moving aside a world of lifetime troubles and woe—a world that included love, but that also included conscious malevolence.

More than anything else, my father was a Black world-conscious Black man who touched and respected Black women in diverse and amazingly tender ways. Going through his papers, I came across a will he had made when he was on his way to Korea, in the event that his death preceded that of "Inola Copelin Ferdinand," his wife. Emotionally more important for me than his will, I discovered a telegram from him and his sons that he sent to my mother wishing her a happy birthday. My father was full of feeling for Black women.

There are many stories I could share about how my father cared for and about Black women. He was not a woman chaser. He was a conscious race man who knew the importance of caring for and about Black women. My own feelings about women have been shaped by his vision. In this day and age, that is a plenty to receive.

My father's world was so emotionally huge. His world

included every Black one of us, both kin and kind, and especially the Black and poor of us. While my father was here, he graced me (and my brothers, and my mother, and many others) with his touch. His touch gave me the strength of mind, body, and most of all, the strength of spirit to carry on.

I can remember my father going to see about my grandfather when I was a young child (about ten years old). At the time, I did not understand why my grandfather lived alone. I knew he was a jackleg preacher. I knew he had worked on the riverfront as a longshoreman, and I knew he did some plumbing work. But I did not know why he lived alone.

To this day, I do not remember one word my grandfather said to or in front of me, but I remember vividly the sense of this man being alone. I would see him moving in the front yard, sometimes sitting out on the porch. I never remember seeing him go anywhere. My father said that White people had run my grandfather out of Napoleonville, which is where they all were from. My grandfather had gotten into an argument with a White man and was going to shoot him with a shotgun. To me, that was a definite plus. So, I wondered about my grandfather and had a generally positive, if puzzled, appreciation of him as a man.

In 1965, I was at Fort Bliss, Texas, in the army. I was not home when Hurricane Betsy hit and flooded New Orleans. Everything was underwater. My grandfather died during the hurricane. They found him after the water receded. He had retreated into a closet and had drowned there.

My brother Kenneth swam over to look for him but could not find him. The water had come up so quickly because the city officials decided to break the levee down in the Ninth Ward in order to save the Downtown area. That's the way a lot of people in the Ninth Ward, where we lived, tell the story.

Emotionally, it was not a big loss to me, but intellectually, his dying without me getting to know him meant something that I grapple with now. How do you recover someone you never knew? My grandfather is gone now, and though he had lived next door, I had not really known him.

I knew that my father felt it important to take care of him, even though my father never said anything about loving or missing my grandfather or anything like that. Yet, by example, my father went out of his way to take care of his father.

When I left Tennessee Street and moved back in with my father, what struck me immediately was not simply the realization that my father lived alone, but the conditions under which he was living. There was something analogous to what I remembered about my grandfather. My father did not have a working stove, and he listened to the radio a lot, mostly to talk shows. He worked at the community center helping with food distribution and other projects, and with senior citizens', groups and he also worked with the NAACP, often using his van to transport folk.

Both my father and grandfather were real Black fathers, and real Black fathers are universally respected and loved in the Black community, no matter their individual limits or short-comings. I do not care what popular sociology* says about Black men as fathers, Black fathers are very special and very important human beings. To be Black, man, and father in modern America is no small accomplishment. Yet, we have had many males among us who have somehow managed to

---

* popular reading of Black reality that starts with non-African premises about social life and hence comes to some logical but erroneous conclusions about African American life.

be all three—something akin to sainthood, except that they are flesh and blood, emotions and thoughts, and uniformly tough.

Both my father's and grandfather's lives helped to shape my vision of family. Family is not only the blood but also the sharing of struggle, conditions, vision, principles, dreams, hardships, food, individual joys, and troubles. We are proud when one member of the family excels or achieves, or conversely sorrowful when a member crosses the law or otherwise falls from grace. As the sharing stops, the family stops.

Given the patterns of life today, beyond the breakup of nuclear family units, the real fissure is within the extended family. Given the fact that moving away from home has now become commonplace, very few of us presently live within (or even want to live within) walking distance of our immediate relatives. How then can we even begin to honestly and realistically talk about family?

This popular sociology, with its unceasing talk about the breakup of the Black nuclear family, is a bunch of junk. It was the extended Black family, not the nuclear family, that carried us across the troubled waters.

Some of us tried to turn our voluntarily formed organizations into extended families, consciously thought of them in that way. At the funeral of a mutual friend, one man said to me as he looked with nostalgic love at a small handful of people he had not seen in years, "At one point, we were all so close to each other, we thought we would never separate, never." He did not finish his thought with words, but his eyes, sad and glazed, bore haunted witness: most of them had not seen each other for years.

No, it was never the mythical nuclear family, it was the extended family that was our bridge across troubled waters. The extended family, which often included people not related by blood but rather by shouldering the responsibility of sharing, was our social glue. In the 70s, we came unstuck and by the year 2000, unless there is a radical change, it will then be all over for the Black extended family in America. And it will be all over for us as a people because to be people, individuals must become extensions of one another, must share with one another.

We cannot be people without extended family. Yet the dominant society demands (and enforces its demand with all kinds of inducements) the breakup of allegiance to anything except individual desire, precisely so that the economic sector can profit from catering to the desires of the individual. Family be damned. Alienation is good for sales.

I know it was Black women who kept us together since slavery. I know when Black men could not be fathers, Black women kept on being mothers. The children stayed with women, were nursed by women—not necessarily their biological mother, but by a woman nonetheless. I know that, if indeed anyone can, it will be Black women as a group who will make the difference. But meanwhile, and in the in-between while, individual Black men will continue to make a significant difference. Black men will be the significant others, especially Black fathers who, by some example—an example that few can predict—will put steel in the backs of young Black men and love in the hearts of young Black women. In the rare case of real, strong Black man/fatherhood, they will put both steel and love into the backs and hearts of both young Black men and women.

We men know the dread of Black manhood, even if no one else knows, even if we never talk about it. We know how ultimately unsuccessful most of us are at being the man we think we ought to be. We know the obstacles to manhood, even when we do not know how those obstacles got in our path. Even worse, we do not know how to get pass those obstacles. Deep inside of us, we men know how hard it is to be a man. We are not fooled by what passes for the trappings of manhood. Degrees and awards do not make a man, nor cars and clothing, women diamonds, money, sitting on various committees and receiving or being a dignitary. We might admire some or all of that. We might strive for or hope to attain most of that. Yet, Black men, deep down, know that those things are not what manhood is about. Black manhood cannot be defined in a few words, but it is easily recognized and easy to love, in fact, almost impossible *not* to love.

At my father's funeral, all three of his sons spoke, starting with the youngest, Keith, continuing through the middle, Kenneth, and ending with the oldest, Kalamu. Part of what I had to say was a recollection. I felt I literally had to tell the assembled mourners some words that I thought expressed some of my father's significance. I recalled a family trip out to California to see my Uncle Pat. It was late at night and we were travelling the last leg of our journey through Arizona. This was in the 50s, still very much a time of hard-line racial segregation. A White man was hitch hiking. My father was driving. We stopped. He asked my mother to drive, he got in the back seat and sat next to the now former hitch-hiker, and we gave the man a ride to the next town. After the man got out, I asked my father why he had given the man a ride. He gave me a simple explanation, the simplicity of which still reverberates inside of me: "It was too late at night for anybody to be out there alone."

I think the 90s are too late at night for any of us to be out there alone.

Sun Song V

remember bobby womack admitting
his pain to the world, or
yrself, remember yrself vowing never, never
never to ever be hurt like that again, vowing
i will never never ever
put myself in a position
to be hurt like that again
remember me, i'm not exempt from this
as i write this poem

we all are seekers
we are all looking, we are
looking, we are looking, we are
looking for love
and yet, oh yes, make no mistake
we most definitely want, need and are
fighting for political power
we'll take some economic development
we'll even go after higher education too,
but what we're really looking for,
especially now that we've gotten older
and are less inclined to believe in material
things...

what can i say abt love
that you have not heard before
that our voices have not cogently wrung from
song lyrics, some lonely
sister has not ached, what can be said
after all is said, nothing, nothing can be said
'cause words won't warm the pillow, and applause
from an audience or awards, well
at night in the apartment alone, the room
dark, yr eyes wide open, what do you thk
that means—a lot of peo. admire
my work and even, and even
even though there are peo.
who love me...this is difficult,
you know what i'm trying to say
how it is when you can't find what you
need, we are all out there, and most of us
are seekers
still looking, still searching,
still in desperate need, and even sometimes
when we get close to it, we are too afraid...

i can't go on w/h this
this shit is too hard...
i'm not going to stop living
i'm not going to stop working
but this shit, this shit
is soooo hard...

A Palace In The Bush

(from a letter to Baraka Sele)

I have been traveling since the sun was straight up and now
it is nearly down. In a more profound sense, I have been
traveling since I first saw the light. The first journey I remember
is crawling on a second-floor balcony. A long flight of blue
stairs led down to the ground. The apartment was on the right
side of the building on Dryades Street. Part of this memory is
confirmed by my parents' address listed on my birth certificate.
I passed the house once. It still had the outdoor staircase.

Once we are born, we start traveling, so, in one sense, this
has been a 43-year journey. Yet, five hours earlier, I had
climbed in the car after filling the tank and headed out to
Houston, intending not to stop until I covered the 300-plus miles
between New Orleans and Houston. So, in another sense, it has
been a five hour journey.

After exiting the freeway, I pulled into a gas station to refill
the empty tank. I was too near where I wanted to be to run
out of gas. I knew why I was traveling: I was tired. I needed
a break. Urban life can be so frustrating. Now that I had gotten
this far with my near-sighted self, I would have to drive more
slowly and look closer and more carefully so I would not get
lost. It's something when you do not know exactly where you
are going even though you are fully committed to going there,
wherever "there" may be. You may know why you are going,

but you do not even have a clue as to what you can realistically expect to find once you are there. You know what you hope to find, but hope is a future thing. Between what you wish for and what you get – well, that can be a trip. In fact, that *is* the trip.

Finally, I am at the door with a watermelon in my hand.

As I enter the open door, I am deep in the bush. You sit waiting, dressed in indigo cloth and a smile. I do not remember your brief words, but your eyes spoke welcome. Leaving my shoes at the doorway, a custom I know, admire, and am very comfortable with, I cross the floor and place the watermelon at your side. There is nothing in the room that a Western-acculturated person would recognize as furniture except rugs and mats on the floor. There is what might have been a table at another time, but now, it is like an altar or something sacred for communicating with spirits. Books are arranged on a rug on the floor. A telephone is built into a wooden pyramid. I am somewhere different. Outside along Spanish and Span-glish wafts along the afternoon breeze. As you move to greet me, there is the gentle jangle of ringing metal. You are wearing miniature bells on your ankle and a row of bangles almost half a forearm long.

We talk quietly, unhurriedly. The phone interrupts us. As you converse with someone on the other end, I ease into the shower, cleanse myself of the road grime, and simultaneously scent my skin with a two-thirds-used bar of translucent Brazilian black rose-fragrance soap. I emerge nude and begin reading until you finish the call. We continue talking, very quietly and with no pressure to finish even one sentence or thought. Our conversation falls like ripe fruit from a tree. Whenever a word is ready, it drops from one of our lips. There are stretches of silence when neither of us is saying anything with our mouths except maybe a noiseless kiss upon the navel or along the crevice beneath where the arm and shoulder meet, or even the delicious recess of the eye socket, skimming a fluttering eyelid. We are in no hurry because the travel is over. Once you have arrived, the only travel left is to complete circles of enjoyment, like a gull floating above a lake occasionally dipping into the water. Our tongues are fluttering wing feathers, our mouths moist, sensual lakes.

On my back, in this place, with the dusk light creeping out of the window, leaving us behind clothed only in nude darkness, I think: none of us knows where we will end up, where life will bring us, but if we are strong, we travel anyway. We go where the flow takes us. If we are trusting, we become friends with all the strangers our travels introduce to us. There is nothing human that is really strange, just maybe "new" to us. If we are wise, we learn to love those who are like us in their love of everything they do not already know.

We talk about ourselves, our people, the future, the disappearance of light, the joy of music, and other important matters before agreeing to exit to eat. Later, we return to this quiet place and I travel deeper into the bush, blessed by your spirit touch. The ambience: the taped Portuguese of Emilo Santiago's soft samba voice, whose lingering tones both accompany and guide our smooth, slow journey, feels like floating. Just hours before, I was driving, walking, using the large muscles of my body, but now, for the most part, rather than straight lines and angles, horsepower and swiftness, now I use slow motion, savoring and tasting, circular movement, redundant touches that are so deeply satisfying; fingertips, brushes with the back of the hand, tongue tips, a bearded cheek rubbed against an erect nipple.

As humans we have our beginnings deep inside the bush, call that bush "womb"—the act of birth is an act of separating self from the world that nurtured us until we were strong enough to stand the light. We all have been babies. We all were conceived in darkness and moved from seed to fetus in the dark liquidity of the womb. That is why we close our eyes when we make love. We are experiencing that bonding of the self with another self at a level where we cannot tell where one self stops and the other self starts; at a level where, with eyes closed we see all kinds of things inside our selves. We feel that we are not where we are, whether it be a bed, floor, or car seat. We are loving (simply fucking will not give us this feeling, nor even the most expert prostitute). All of that is a perversion of the love union, which is but a momentary recapturing of the womb experience. We close our eyes because, at that moment, we do not need light to see all there is to see. All that matters at that moment—no matter how brief or fleeing that moment—is that moment. That moment we seek, that moment that many of us seldom find, not even in our dreams, the moment that once we find we never forget. That moment.

I have been traveling a long time, and now I am here. Because I realize that there is nowhere in the world as warm as the original womb, no lasting spot of satisfaction, because I realize the temporalness of peace outside the womb, when I find the milli-moment in the midst of day-to-day madness, I shut down the engines and float through it, gliding on the inertia of saudaude (a Brazilian word for nostalgia in the most profound sense, slave & post/neo-slave longing for Africa, or even more profoundly, human longing for the womb, for true peace). The great contradiction of life is that nothing alive stands still; everything expands and contracts. The process of living is expansion. The process of dying is contraction. Although we are born in the womb, as soon as we live we begin growing. It is life itself that forces us out the womb, our own growing that exceeds what the womb is able to hold. In the post-womb world, we grow past what our bodies are able to sustain; the physical begins to deteriorate because it has lived beyond the time period of sound molecular structure. Like a child's top—spinning and spinning, a brilliant blur but eventually slowing, and slowing, and finally falling over—we are spinning. The top is still until the moment the child throws it and pulls the string. Until our umbilical c(h)ords are cut, we are tops in the creator's hand. Then the string is pulled and we spin until we slow down and stop. In some cases, we misfire and spin out of control. Sometimes, when a number of people are playing a vicious game of tops, a spinning top is attacked by another spinning top, or someone picks it up and plays with it. (I am on my back thinking this, you are sucking my nipple, and I am sent spinning into another world. How else could I think of this?)

Once we are born, the only environment in which we can survive is in the light, outside the womb's darkness. That unquenchable, simultaneous desire to live and to return to the beginning is not exactly a desire for death. It is a desire for pre-birth. It is a desire for something dimly remembered, a desire that is so ephemeral, most of us do not even consciously know we are seeking the security of the womb. Yet, it is a desire so powerful that even our consciousness is unable to deter or stop this spiritual quest for the pre-birth state. Once we are born, this quest can only be momentarily fulfilled by experiences of love. Ultimately this desire can be fulfilled only by death.

Some intellectuals believe sex is like death. They are wrong. Sex is like pre-birth, like the womb. After we are born, the closest we can come to the womb is either love or death. Unlike the ecstasy of coital union, which is so brief even though it is so sharp, death is a lasting affair. In that way, death is the only darkness close to the security of the womb. This instinctual fight to stay alive is poised against the urge to get back to the origins, to the womb. This urge can only be fulfilled by death, by exiting from this world. Indeed to live, to be born, is to die, is to experience the "death" of expulsion from the womb.

Sometimes we search for years, sometimes we do not even know to look, nor do we realize what is missing in our lives. Most of us never find "dar es salaam" (place of peace). We rarely find even a moment of peace, except perhaps in our artistic expressions and in love. It is like the transcendence we feel with music that connects us with others. Even in the audience, even though not the musician, when the music is really on, we are swept up and transported to a place the believers call "heaven" (dar es salaam). Mystics talk about meditating to achieve this state, but much of that is just self-hypnosis because it is a journey alone. With music and with love, more than one can go at a time. We can travel together.

The womb is life inside of life, the bonding of one life inside another. The womb is not an individual place; there are always at least two. I have learned that I cannot re-enter the womb. But, as long as I am alive, I can be true to myself, my molecular structure, my cultural groundings, my dreams, my potential as a human, myself. So now, I travel in search of the self, not the womb, but to achieve the full development of the self which began in the womb. Even though I have this nostalgia, this *saudaude* for the womb, I also understand that I can never return there. But before I stop spinning and fall over, I must spin out a rainbow. I must be myself.

When my arms are around you, I am not thinking these thoughts. In fact, sometimes I am not thinking at all. But when I remember holding you and being held by you, when remembering love, it makes me think about this and much more. Love enables me to recognize the awesomeness of the universe.

While I wax philosophical, I also respond emotionally, and respond from a deep past. As much as I am a traveler like so many others are travelers, at this moment I am different. I have been blessed with the real-world expression of dreams I had as an adolescent reading books and thinking about my life as an adult. Here, on a tender evening of my life, I am wise enough to bend to smell the flowers. I could be elsewhere, but I am here, laying on the floor, naked, my arms at my side, completely at peace. Inside the palace in the bush, I find myself. I find myself and laugh a silent laugh. For here I am deep in the bush of blackness, a Black woman beside me, and I am at peace.

Approaching the end of the 20th century, America is disintegrating, self-destructing. The world is being disrupted by aliens. Most of us spend our lives working for someone else, at jobs that will not improve the quality of our lives one iota. Most of us are terribly inefficient when it comes to achieving satisfying relationships. At best, most of us are survivors. Yet, we zoom on through, sometimes faking that we are more secure than we actually are. We pretend we are happier than we are, and even when we be sad and talk bad about ourselves and the world, we do not fully register the terrible thought that we have done nothing of value. In the process of living, we have lost ourselves. We do not even know who we are anymore. Caught in the currents of the mainstream, we dress, eat, wear our hair, look at each other, talk about each other, and decorate the spaces where we live—just like our tormentors. As a result of living day-to-day aping aliens, we do not even know ourselves. We end up spending long days and nights away from ourselves, and it is a tough journey to get back.

I have been traveling a long time. There are people on the road behind me who are disappointed by some of my motions. (Moving away from people who would rather that you and they travel together is always disappointing.) We humans are imperfect travelers. Even those of us who try hard to move gracefully, and especially those of us who try to make a difference, we hurt others. But like sharks who, by their nature, must move constantly or die, we who would change the world can be terribly destructive as we pursue our goals. We leave in our wake the shattered and scattered hopes of those who tried to hold us, tried to love us. Movement cannot be held. You can move with motion but you cannot hold it. By our nature, artists and activists are unstable, constantly in motion, constantly reaching and constantly hurting those who want to hold to us. Ask anyone who has ever loved (ever tried to love) an activist or artist and they will tell you the tales of the futility of trying to stand motion still. It would be a lie to say I regret being the way I am or that I wish I was another way. I am happy to be me, even though I must wage a constant battle with those who would have me not be me. This battle is a struggle that sometimes inadvertently, yet inevitably, hurts people who love me.

Yes, I have been traveling a long time, and that long time traveling has been more painful than not. So, sometimes I slow down to a trot or an amble and rest on the run. Oh, this mad spinning world, this top we cling to. Oh these streets and emotions we navigate. Oh, this bright blackness in a world uniformly covered by manipulators who disdain colors. Oh, this America, this social structure. This is not normal. Mistakes and mess ups are normal. America is not normal. And in the midst of dedicating my life to making change, to creating my writing, I often find myself looking for rest even though I know I can never stop.

So here I am, in this place, this palace, this "official" residence. In this case, "official" does not mean the state but rather the soul, the hideaway, the place where the maroon can reside outside of the reach of the state. I am momentarily at peace, but still my mind is moving. The time is passing. I have but so many hours allotted to be here. Even if I could afford to stay longer, that longer would not really be much longer. Do you know that the person sprawled before you is simply slowed motion and can never be fully at rest?

I have been traveling for a long time. All of us have, although most of us never think about it. I look up at the ceiling, and feel myself relaxing. I don't wish for this to last forever. Instead, I give thanks that I have found this at all. I take what I can get. I have been traveling, and now, lying in a candle-lit room, I am blessed. My journey through the world has brought me to this palace in the bush, inside which I find myself, on the floor at midnight, anointed with a kiss, looking down at my natural self from the vantage point of the mountain of dues I have paid along the road. I discover this journey is ultimately simply about self-definition.

Since we cannot return to the womb, neither out of a longing for that pre-birth state nor out of a desire to change the way we are (our color, our station in life, our sex), all we can do is be what we are. For people of color in America, the struggle to be what we are is a supreme effort precisely because being what we are goes against the mainstream of America. All our lives, our travel is either back into the bush or else down the road of forgetfulness—the road of assimilation and otherness that diminishes our own selfness, truncating all our differences and forcing our big butts into flat trousers. Otherwise, life travel is a dangerous journey swimming against the current, without map, without compass, without anything except heart and a belief that "the sun gon' shine in my back door someday." Life travel is a steady moving forward fueled by whatever our personal resources are and by our faith in our mothers, fathers, ancestors, children, and ultimately, ourselves. That is how we travel, those of us who do not accept assimilation into the status quo. And it is a hard journey to get out of the entrails of whiteness.

On this road, we do not find rest until we are at one with ourselves. There can be no rest until we find the path away from our captors, a path along which there are many cul de sacs. I have been traveling a long time, and like many others, when I started out I did not fully realize what all of this would mean in the long run, nor how arduous this journey would be. I did not know that being myself is not only a search for self, but also a battle for my life. A fight with those who would stop me from being me. Daily, the journey requires I fight those whose political and economic interests demand my ignorance. I did not even know that this was where I was going, but I have an inner sense that knows far more than my mind knows. So when at last I am back into the bush of myself, back where the inclination is to be natural—be myself—I respond instinctively when my path crosses the path of another runaway. And at that moment, just before I fall asleep, the sweetest lesson is realized: no matter how much of the world they may control, the interior of our souls—the bush belongs to us.

Give Thanx.

Sun Song VI

the air is black

outside yr window, now,
up above yr head, you perceive
blueness, or at least clouds,
a sun, moon or stars,
& beyond that
in the religion of yr imagination, heaven
or some variant thereof, but this
is the tail end of the 20th
century, & you
need a machine to hear the air

a receiver of some sort:
television, a satellite dish, a radio
or better yet a boom box - portable,
not just a receiver but also a player

when you listen to the air
really listen, the evidence is irrefutable
you know down to yr tapping toe,
whoever you be, wherever you go,
you know
the air is black

black with the rhythms and melodies
of displaced africans transformed
  by time and circumstance, reharmonizing

the discordant jangle of the empire
imploding, the sound of the center
unable to hold

all modern music is us, or directly
influenced by what we have done

even c&w at its whitest
remains at root level nothing more
than cleverly worded, poor white tales
inspired by gospel, blues and r&b

the scottish klan descendants of blue-
grass picked the banjo as their instrument
of choice, the banjo, a string instrument
appropriated by europeans shortly after
its first appearance as "banja" bamboula tool
but, just like you don't see how the air sounds
many people don't see the roots & reality
of modern culture, they see sun and stars
but not the sociology and political
economy of sounds, how the owners and
controllers of culture are not the true creators,
the difference between consciousness and acculturation
is lost on a public that can't read
the reality of the videos they see and
can't hear what's not being said, oh so sad
are the emotional skinheads (especially
the ones with long hair) who love blk music
 but only when its played by whites

why are americans so hung up
on race, so many citizens of this nation
embracing our music while distancing themselves

from we the people, a people they created
by dragging us into a mulatto culture
which is psychologically incapable of accepting
the colors of its conception, orphaning
any of its issue which cannot metamorphize
into the whiteness of racism's self
induced immaculate deceptions

they want our music
but they don't want we the people,
they want to dance like us
but not dance with us
        (xcept, of course, as some exotic other,
        some titillating erotic, a rite of passage
        into adulthood: "oh yes
        one had their tongue down my throat once,
        & wet all in my ear, always, in my ear
        and i can't forget that
        feeling, i kinda got off on that")

oh, if only we all could,
even if for just
the briefest of moments, could
just get and go beyond, beyond
our education, our socializations,
and definitely beyond
the limits sight imposes,

if we all could sing,
or at least pat our foot
and keep time, all of us
conditioned by this
modern world would
recognize the obvious:

the air we breathe
and need
to live

the air

is black,
black
and beautiful

FISH OUT OF WATER

A Reaction to the New
Charles Lloyd CD On ECM

#117
fish out of water
art shot from the bow of gods
we rise above self

After the music, we all want a better world. The music extends our imagination, sensitizes our feel for life's possibilities, heightens our desire for an end to ugliness, creates an awareness of the infinite non-necessity of destruction. Things fly apart on their own. Nature does not need our help. Besides, more often than not, human "help" is actually a hindrance to the natural order of dissolution. Dissolution always leads to rebirth in the natural state, with every death being the matrix of another life form. Even excrement fertilizes fields.

After the music, we understand all of this better. Well, not really understand. All enlightenment teaches us is how much we do not know. The struggle is to say yes to art for life and no to death. Yes, I will leave this world better and more beautiful than when I arrived. I will give more than I take. I will help more than I hurt.

The struggle is really to rise above ourselves.

Charles Lloyd. Fish out of water. Be of the world and yet

leave it behind, even if but for only the briefest moment. Be the art/arrow of a creator piercing the depths of mundanity with a flaming arc aimed toward the distant target always just beyond our human reach. We may never strike the bull's eye, but we should never fail to aim.

We do not eat the fish. We eat the image of the fish flying, and our souls are filled with the imagined flying of our own fish features. Rather than the fish's flesh, we taste the leap of the fish. The aftertaste teaches us that we too can leap above ourselves. We can leap above ourselves.

When we sight the fish out of water, we envision our own selves maintaining the incredible way-outness of that moment in the atmosphere. Although we are away from our fishy nature, we are essentially still ourselves, just momentarily our better selves. Once there, we will want to remain there, or, at the very least, visit there very frequently. Music raises your aspirations above base level.

Charles Lloyd: "I am an arrow."

This new record is so calming, a quiet *woosh*, arcing through the dawn air. We follow its rainbow radiance into ourselves to discover that the target is not a thing but a process. This process moves us away from being overly concerned with self, from being mundane, from pain, from inflicting or being afflicted by pain.

The music is not mellow. It does not inspire one to lounge around or to engage in a romantic tryst. This music eschews the pleasures of the flesh. Not out of disdain for the physical, it is just that, at this moment, the mission is somewhere else. Going beyond the boundaries is what this expression is about.

Going beyond the boundaries takes both heart and more than heart. Heart is love, but heart is also courage.

Going beyond the boundaries requires you to love your nature and love being yourself. First, you must love being alive. But then, in order to move so that the love of self does not lead to total selfishness, you must accept the challenge of living a good life. You must do this even when others make it easier for you to kill or die, even when the society makes it seem like there are only two life options: exploiting others or being exploited by others. The whole point, however, is that exploitation, whether inflicting it or having it inflicted upon you, is a barrier, and our goal is life beyond exploitation.

As inescapable as exploitation may seem in this century and in this world, we can literally overcome it simply by living and helping others to live. How else could we African Americans have created our culture? Our culture is not a slave culture but a culture of human aspiration for far loftier goals than material acquisition and social dominance. We have always wanted to live. Further, we have always known that no matter the hand we are dealt we can choose to live a good life, even if living the good life requires us to become martyrs.

Living is always an act of expansion, of going beyond what is. Dying is an act of diminishment, of accepting and eventually being overwhelmed by the restrictions of existence. To truly live is to constantly move, learn, and grow. To die is to do just the opposite. If you are self-satisfied, you are on the verge of death.

There is no reward for living a good life except experiencing a life well lived. That state is so beautific that it is more than ample reward for whatever trials one must endure to achieve the well-lived life. Moreover, living well is not something anyone can do for you or to you. Living well is a process of challenging yourself to move past whatever confinements and restrictions are placed on you by circumstance and society.

Although it is metaphysical to simply think about living well, whether one is Harriet Tubman, Sojourner Truth, Malcolm X, or Martin Luther King—an artist, social organizer, mystic, or an activist—if one actually lives well, then one has attained all that is possible for any of us to attain.

When one aims beyond the boundaries, the trip itself is the destination. Because we are human and live in the real world, there are always boundaries. Because we are also spirit, we can always strive to go beyond. Of the water, born in the water, fly out the water, fall back in the water, fly out of the water, die in the water—water creatures nevertheless, but with a spirit that transcends wateriness.

Make no mistake, there is nothing metaphysical about living well in a world gone commercially mad. Living well is indeed a struggle, as any walk down any street will make perfectly clear. Love alone is insufficient to change reality. Love in the abstract is ineffective. What is required is the courage to appear foolish in the eyes of the material world. One needs courage to be someone who does not care about money. (As in we care, but we have our priorities, and we care more about life than money.) One needs courage to travel alone (even when we crave social contact, social approval, and social reinforcement).

While others sleep or swim, it takes courage to fly. The sleepers and the swimmers will not only tell you that flying is a sin, that it is impossible, but the moment you leave the water, they will become (consciously or unconsciously, actively or passively) part of the gravity trying to pull you back down. Indeed, our nature as fish will not allow us to stay out of the water for very long, even when we do manage to fly.

Ultimately, the infiniteness of struggle in our lifetime notwithstanding, no barrier is impermeable if we have the courage to completely expose our selves in our quest to go beyond the boundaries. And whenever we go, whether we desire to or not, the nature of this travel demands that we travel light. We can only enter the higher realms naked and vulnerable, totally exposed to reactionary forces who may actually be offended by our audacity in exposing the nude and unarmed soul; totally exposed to exploitative forces who are looking for fish to eat.

Charles Lloyd's music helps me to think about all of this by creating an atmosphere that invites reflective thought—his art is a breeze that helps move us along (although it is left to the listener to stretch her or his own wings). Charles Lloyd does not think for you, he just creates an atmosphere conducive to thought. His music is canvas and colors. You must make the brushstrokes.

On an aural plane, this music offers the opportunity to merge the physical and the spiritual. There is a duality in the music: rhythm (physicality) and lyricism (spirituality). The rhythm makes you dance. The lyricism impels you to flight. The music makes you believe. The wingless soul flies. You dance on air.

I believe in life, in reality, but I do not for one moment believe there is anything better than art in life, than the artful rearranging of life. I sincerely believe there is no vocation better than making life more beautiful and much better than when we arrived on the scene. For me, of all the arts, music is the purest and least encumbered expression of emotion.

What is life without music? Fish imprisoned in water not simply by gravity or inertia, but really by their own inability or unwillingness to imagine themselves flying!

This message was inspired by the music of that Memphis-born mystic, Charles Lloyd. Give thanks & praises. Amen-RA.

OUTSIDE:

the Beat / Rhythm of Being

Sun Song VII

the Portuguese found it
hard to believe that there
was a woman leading this resistance
pushing them back toward the sea

the Portuguese wondered
when she menstruated or cried
maybe she was a stone virgin
who never "succumbed to man"

this fighting woman
did not square with the females
they had left behind
their vaginas locked in chains

didn't their breasts get in
the way of arms?
how could woman be so effective
hand to hand?

one young soldier stood and died dumb,
uncontrollably soiling himself
as the sharp spear entered
and exited his bowels

there fell a young man
who could not comprehend the reality,
except by personal death experience,
that women can be warriors

women can be warriors

If the Hat Don't Fit,
How Come We're Wearing It?

An Appreciation of Women Writing

I f the hat don't fit, how come we're wearing it is not a question but a statement. When African American men question the contemporary writings of African American women, they are not really questioning aesthetics, politics, form, structure, or content. What is really evidenced is a pained reaction: a statement of hurt, perhaps envy, and certainly an automatic defense of the walking-wounded, male ego.

Sometimes when the sisters turn up the heat, we brothers retreat into sullen silence, pull the wool over our eyes, wrap our ears in mufflers, and don huge fur caps which totally cover our heads (even in summer). We do all of this allegedly to "protect" ourselves from the bad weather. But what bad weather? Do we really need to be protected from the writings of African American women? Many men do not even want to deal with the writings of contemporary African American women in general, and writers like Shange, Walker, Lorde, Morrison specifically.

Like swingers stumbling on the rhythms of bebop, like a self-proclaimed alto saxophonist who has just figured out Bird's (Charlie Parker) "Donna Lee" being confronted with the white plastic, smoldering bent notes of Ornette Coleman's "Lonely Woman," like anyone comfortably bound in tradition then confronted with a future which is difficult to fathom, we blame the drummer when we cannot catch the rhythm. The reality is that we just do not understand what our sisters are writing nor why. Moreover, we really do not want to go through the changes of learning how to read this music. "Besides," we think to ourselves, "what is there to gain from understanding a difficult woman when we can find easy ones?" For us "easy" means a feminine voice that is content to be a period at the end of our sentences rather than a troublesome question mark challenging us.

SISTERS ARE THROUGH BLOWING ALL THE THINGS MEN ARE

No matter how hip bop was, there was still much more music left to be made. Music not only new but also different. Like Trane, tired of playing "All the Things You Are" over and over again with only minute melodic variations, many sisters have abandoned the old song forms and are sounding out new song forms. "Favorite Things" no longer sounds like anything we recognize.

When the new music hit, a lot of the establishment could not hear it. "Anti-jazz" is what they called Dolphy and Trane. An immensely important artifact like "Meditations" was rated "no stars" in *Downbeat* by a critic with lead in his ears. Likewise, brothers close their minds to sisters' songs, complaining about the noise and crying about how bad the sisters write about us.

For example, somebody always brings up Ntozake Shange's image of the brother dropping the baby out the window. Dudes be enraged, saying Shange is a menace to men, a divisive force in the Black community who pits the women against the men. These same brothers rarely utter one word against Wright's *Native Son*. They do not mention how Bigger took a big brick and bashed Bessie's brains out 'cause she—Black and female and in his arms when he got mad—had nerve enough to love him.   Cats do not mention Trueblood in *Invisible Man,* unashamed of his acts of incest.   Don't mention the male character in Baraka's play *Madheart,* the character who slaps the Black woman and beats her to the stage floor as part of her "revolutionary" instruction. I mean, what have women looked like in much of what we have written?

The writings of women are easily understandable as a counterweight to the imbalance of past literature. But actually, these new songs are more than the past, much more than simply reactions to the traditional AABA popular song form ("A" being male, "B" being female). When Ornette cut "The Shape of Things to Come," he wasn't trying to rewrite history. Rather, he was shaping the future. Ditto what the sisters are doing. The past is gone. Regardless of how many of us may want to hold on to out-moded ideas, since the sisters blew through with their new songs, things will never be the same. Never. And thank goodness!

It is both dishonest and untrue to say that the "negative male" characters presented by sisters are atypical or unrealistic. Traditionally, men have been socialized to demonstrate and condone anti-female behaviors and attitudes.   Through its persuasive and pervasive media network, the men who run this society constantly reinforce a negative and/or subordinate view of women. With or without knowledge of the social forces at work, every man who is not actively struggling against sexism is either actively promoting or passively supporting sexism just by accepting the status quo.

Being a man in modern American has been a position of privilege and dominance vis-a-vis women. This is the case regardless of the feelings and actions of individual women and men that may vary from the norm of female/male relationships. It is this hard fact of life, this business as usual, that is rightly being criticized. Bigger and all similar-acting brothers are indefensibly wrong in their social relationships with women.

Objectively, if some of us are not Bigger-like in our social relationships, why should we feel any heat about the negative portraits of Bigger-ish behavior? To assert that most men are not like Bigger avoids confronting the reality of day-to-day life: most men have the potential to be Bigger-like, and this society traditionally encourages such behavior.

Upon close study, it is clear that women's male characters are written far more realistically than men's female characters. Undoubtedly, it is only our male blindness, defensiveness, and possibly chauvinistic self-interest that prevents us from understanding and accepting the figurative and literal validity of male characters portrayed in the contemporary works of African American female writers.

If the cap don't fit, then why are we wearing it? Why are we insisting that there is something so wrong with conscious and critical women writing true-to-life stories about how men routinely treat women in our culture?

In African American literature of the 60s, it was common to find the image of women as "mirrors" of "their men." Now that the mirror talks and says what she sees, all of a sudden we are pronouncing the image distorted and contending that the mirror is blemished. Have we men ever considered that perhaps the blemish lies not in the mirror, but in the subject, in the male?

This is not to say that the works of women are perfect in both execution and content. There is much to criticize, but the fact that African American men have colluded with the sexist status quo remains true. Generally, we men materially and psychologically have advanced ourselves via male domination of women. Women who point out and criticize this central truth can hardly be accused of hating men and promoting divisiveness. There is nothing wrong with criticizing one's conditions.

Most men are not ready to take the cap off, even though some of us are willing to chivalrously "tip" our caps to those women whom we recognize as "ladies." Fortunately, women are through smiling at the emperor's old cap.

LIKE TONI C. SAID, "NOBODY ASKED YOU TO LIKE IT"

Some of us men are slick. Inside of certain relationships we remove our caps; but otherwise, we hold our caps in our laps and reserve the right to put them on whenever we feel like doing so. We only condemn certain "female" writers, the ones we consider "too out" (i.e., mainly any woman who is not publicly heterosexual and preferably in a relationship with a Black man). We become liberals on the issue of sexism. We oppose raw sexism but remain unwilling to deal with the subtler but nonetheless destructive aspects of our own chauvinist behavior.

But it is not enough for us men to move pass a vagina fixation. It is not enough to exorcise the "dog" in us. We must also move past a breast fixation. Too many of us want every woman to be our personal nurturer, offering us her breast. We want women to coddle and pet us like cute puppies.

Divorce is up. Rape is up. Pornography is up. Wife-beating and other forms of battering are on the rise. With this reality of the world facing African American women, why should any man expect women to write pleasing portraits of us? Besides which, how would any rational woman define a "pleasing" male?

Whether we men want to see it or not, this world is terribly violent toward women—*forty-eight hours* a day. Did you see that flick? Did you see how the women were presented? You cannot go to the movies today without seeing a woman shot, raped, fucked-over, or socked in the jaw with a fast-swinging male's fist breaking her lip to the accompanying applause of an audience that emotionally agrees with artistic misogyny. In *A Boy and His Dog,* a woman was actually eaten (for survival's sake of course), and that film was set in the year 2000-plus. According to Hollyweird, 20 or so years from now, men and dogs will be casually cannibalizing women.

Look at life through the eyes of a woman and you will see an arsenal of weapons arrayed against you and potential violence from every male you meet. A daughter moving through puberty cannot even trust her father as she steps out the bathtub; she better keep the door locked. Better believe it; momma's top incisor tooth ain't loose 'cause she bit on a bone while eating a steak.

And when it ain't violence, it's sex. Raw. Unrealistic. Heavy breathing from the radio, bump and grind on the television, and triple Xs (XXX) outselling everything on cable. Imagine life as a woman. Then write it like you see it, like you feel it, like it is. Guess how it will come out.

In the final analysis, women writers would not be accurately dealing with their condition if unreconstructed (men who refuse to admit their sexist socialization and are actively anti-feminist in their modes of behavior) males "liked" and applauded the bulk of contemporary writings by women. Just as we did not expect racist Whites to like the Black Arts movement, no one should expect male chauvinists to like anti-sexist writing, even when it is authored by a male, but especially when authored by a female. Most African American women writing today have long ago come to that conclusion. Both the validity of their work and their own will and ability to continue working is in no way dependent on men liking or approving of women's literature.

BUT IS IT JAZZ?

Moreover, it does not really matter what most of us think. Like the Association for the Advancement of Creative Musicians playing to an audience of eight in some hall on Chicago's southside, or Coltrane ascending with Pharaoh even as die-hard fans walked out 'cause they couldn't dig it, the hard fact is that our sisters are going to keep writing.

Contrary to a popular belief, men do not own writing. We men cannot stop women from writing, nor can we dictate content or censor them without becoming Black/male fascists. The very act of wielding our censorial whips and chains suffocates our own humanness in a box inaccurately marked "mankind"—a box that inexorably becomes an auction block and trading station, from which men speculate on the commodities of women's lives, loves, and dreams. We cannot close the mouths of women without first closing our hearts, minds, and spirits. To stop women, we must first stop ourselves from being human. No human being loves oppression. Brave humans fight for freedom. And any person worthy of being called a man would fan the flames of women's struggle to liberate themselves from the tyranny of male chauvinism.

When men say certain women writers/editors "have to be stopped," all we're doing is repeating the drawing-room conversation of plantation owners whom we serve and, unfortunately, too often imitate. The bourgeois—those who possess the major productive forces in this society—always fear any new phenomenon that they do not own or control. In many cases we reject the writings of women not just because we don't like the content, but also because we can't control it. Besides, like a slave rebellion on a nearby farm, this thing could get out of hand and exert a bad influence on our women. Harriet Tubman's coming!

If anything, we ought to encourage sister writers. Let's water this new literature, herald its coming, and look forward to a wider variety of vegetables and fruit. Let's look forward to a far nicer, spicier, and yes, healthier meal than the bogus bread, blood, meat, sugar, and salt diet that most of us imbibe and chase down with alcoholic drinks.

Yes, the new music was really music. Albert Ayler and Archie Shepp are Great Black Music, African Diasporan aural creators using our ear canals to clear our heads. They could blow the standards but chose to set new standards. Our music and our lives are better because they blew what they knew to be real, regardless of what the experts had to say.

Similarly, our lives are better because Toni Cade Bambara, Sonia Sanchez, Mari Evans, Jayne Cortez, Toni Morrison, Alexis DeVeaux, Alice Walker, Maya Angelou, Ntozake Shange, and others are working literature into new areas. Their human geographics not only describe us, but also, and more importantly, women's writings decisively contribute to the voicing of our collective reality. Their voices specifically include previously omitted parts of our history, present, and future. Rather than describing to others/aliens what we are like, African American women are voicing the Black experience, and dialoguing with the folk—field folk, that is, those brave enough to run for it ("it" being hard freedom in the hills).

At the fifth Howard University Writer's Conference, I spoke about what I believe is the wonderful development of women writers. Part of what I said bears reiteration:

> [I]t is my perception and my belief that much of the most creative and politically-important work happening in current Black literature is being authored by women. It may seem that there are more women being published. Overall, the work of talented Black women is more interesting, confronts our conditions in more creative ways, asks more questions, proposes more alternatives to the status quo than do the works of men.
>
> In my opinion, Alice Walker's *The Color Purple*, Toni Bambara's *The Salt Eaters*, Alexis DeVeaux's book on Billie Holiday, and a number of other examples of fiction by Black females are much more inventive than recent published fiction by Black male writers.
>
> Why do I believe this? First, because more of our talented male writers have been, shall we say, "gainfully employed" in status quo positions by colleges, corporations, foundations, and government agencies. More men have received grants, fellowships, and the like. For many Black men, it is no longer in our interest to sink the ship of state because many of us have been granted a berth aboard the U.S.S. Status Quo. Sure, our security aboard ship is shaky, but the point is that we are there, not in the water.
>
> This is a generalization, but I think it is a generalization that corresponds in many important ways to our current reality vis-a-vis our creative writings.

. . . . .

In the context of Black literature, women and those who

are sensitive to women are offering critiques of society that stretch beyond class and race, and this stretching is both healthy and necessary. Female authors are making these important creative strides because they are reacting both to our people's oppression and exploitation in general and to their own particular oppression and exploitation as women. In other words, they are fulfilling their historic mission as articulated by Franz Fanon.

WE GOT TO MOVE

Women writers are not aliens, nor should their presence be surprising. Women writers are truly our colleagues, and we ought to be their comrades. We ought to share struggle and space with them. To do this, we must leave the estates of our male mansions. We must leave the familiar but alien colonial capitals and journey into the bush of ourselves.

Of course, the bush is no easy place to go, especially for those of us who have grown accustomed to the creature comforts of the big cities. The bush can be exhausting, dangerous, and, at times, unmerciful. Yet, the bush is also liberating. The bush is the internal terrain for which we alone are responsible. It is the hearts and imaginations of our people; the now deformed and malnourished center of our existence, which requires not only discovery but also therapy in order to restore whole communities.

Going into the bush requires sacrifice; you cannot ride in air-conditioned splendor. Why go after ephemeral and uncertain freedom in the hills when there are certain comforts to be had beneath the reign of our historic oppressors? The answer is simple: our future is in the bush; the plantation will not survive. We have no choice. Either save ourselves or perish with our oppressors. Essentially, this is what sisters are saying. What do they gain by remaining the wives, bitches, and whores of men's dreams? Look at the reality: many of our sisters are living alone with their children anyway. The social landscape is not improving. That is why more and more of them are running for the hills, running for their lives. And we should be on the road with them, fleeing an oppressive past, escaping to an arduous but liberated future.

Our sisters are not hiding from us, unless, of course, we hold a chain in our hand and are scouts and slave-catchers for the old regime. Our sisters are not begging, requesting, pleading, nor even any longer willing to cross the burning sand and softly present their case at our feet like peasants petitioning a governor. From here on out, if we are to talk, it will be as equals. Dialogue with Black women can only take place when and if we decide that we are willing to leave the big house and live in the hills. Jamaican Maroon leader, Nanny, catches British bullets in her teeth. No way is she going to listen to the bullshit of some *assimilatto* who refers to himself and the establishment as "we."

The women are not waiting for us. They gone. And that's one of the reasons why much of their literature is so interesting.

Sun Song VIII

a system of thot

*we must survive we must
survive we
must survive death
to
the system*

Impotence Need Not Be Permanent

The Decline of Black Men Writing

W ELL, SHUT MY MOUTH.
Who silenced the Black male writer?
Po' boy did it to himself.

Within the dynamics of contemporarily respected social intercourse, many of us Black male writers feel sexually inadequate. To even raise the question of "who silenced Black male writers?" is in fact an admission of inadequacy because the implicit assumption is that we (or most Black male writers) share the view that we have been silenced.

This "silencing question" is multifaceted: (1) We assume that our silence is an impediment to our fulfillment as male writers; (2) although unable to fully identify the culprit, we believe we have been coerced into this involuntary silence; and (3) we are certain that the silencing was done by someone other than ourselves.

But I believe these assumptions conceal the truth. First, if "silenced" means that either we are intellectually incapable of coping with our conditions (and thus have been over-whelmed and resultantly rendered speechless), or that we have been forced by others to say nothing about our current state, then we have not really been silenced. Second, to the degree that we are silent, we have done it to ourselves more than we have been silenced by others. But fear not, like many forms of impotence, our speech impediment problem is in part psycho-socially based, and it can be cured.

The hardest part of dealing with this problem is 'fessin' up, confessing where the problem lies. Moreover, admitting our own inadequacy vis-a-vis women is not easy, especially when we men perceive ourselves as besieged and censored, and also believe that women writers are enjoying "favored writers" status. To hear some of us tell it, rather than the general behavior of men toward women, it is "malicious, angry, and spiteful women who have given manhood a bad name." Others of us are just plain confused: "What," we incredulously ask, "is wrong with being a man?" Although we phrase the question as though we do not understand why we are under siege, that is not the question we are really asking. What we really want to know is "what is wrong with *me* being a man?"

To a frighteningly large extent, many of us men have convinced ourselves that it is our gender per se rather than our behavior that women perceive as the central problem. Just as many Whites convinced themselves that they were being attacked because of their race rather than because of their behavior, many of us men have taken the defensive posture that a feminist critique is preposterous. How could we possibly stop being men? Preposterous or not, we do recognize that there is a serious problem. We hold forums not only to address "the problem" but also hoping to commiserate with one another via an intellectual male-bonding ritual of collective denial.

"YOU CAN HAVE ME BABY / BUT MY LOVIN' DAYS ARE THROUGH"

Let's look at the real problem, rather than the perceived ones. Regardless of sex (or sexual orientation), the intellectual who cannot speak is impotent. The intellectual whose words are ignored is frustrated. The intellectual whose print and broadcast access is severed is castrated. At a gut perceptual level (i.e., what we feel is true), to one degree or another, all of the above describe many Black male writers. Impotent. Frustrated. Castrated. The real question, however, is: who is doing what to whom? How? Why?

The impotence of the Black male is grounded in the complex nexus of exploitation and oppression, and in our individual (re)actions within that context. Within the general social schema, a combination of two major foci immobilize Black male tongues:

1.   We suddenly find ourselves branded the enemy.
2.   We abandoned independent action (i.e., self-deter-mined and self-supported alternatives to the status quo) for failed attempts at integration into the mainstream.

Of these two foci, only the first can, in any remote way, be said to be caused by women. The idea that manhood is the enemy is precisely the arena within which we feel most vulnerable. The majority of Black male writers who feel vulnerable on this issue are either heterosexuals or closet homosexuals. Self-affirmative Black gay writers do not feel as isolated, principally because they are not isolated. They recognize their common condition as gays oppressed by the status quo and are struggling against the status quo both for self-definition and self-respect.

But for those of us who are openly heterosexual or secretly and self-ashamedly homosexual (which generally manifests itself as exaggerated "manliness"), the question is: What are we struggling for? With what movements and what individuals do we identify?

Our problem is that we have no definition of manhood other than that of "man as conqueror." The majority of male-respected definitions of manhood are based not simply on triumphing, but rather on dominating (out-ranking the competition). Additionally, the concept of conqueror almost invariably leads to its logical extension: the concept of oppressor. Before we know it, despite our protestations to the contrary, being a man becomes synonymous with being an oppressor.

Not only do the vast majority of us clearly define our manhood by our ability to dominate in the social arenas of life, but within the generally accepted definition of manhood, the distance between dominator and oppressor is nil. In America, being "The Man" equals being dominant in whatever field of endeavor—sports, business, music, entertainment, education, etc. In the African American vernacular, to be "The Man" means to dominate the scene.

Check this interesting aside: Prince. Even though there are numerous rumors about his alleged (bi)sexuality/androgyny, still he is seen as dominating the pop music scene in terms of the popularity of his product. As long as he dominates (sells), his alleged deviance is tolerable.

"Man as dominator" is precisely the concept under attack. We attack the White man for dominating us, and Black women attack the Black male for being "sexist" (trying to be as dominant, as the "real" man). The upshot of all this is our own particularly cruel cul de sac: not only does the White man dominate us, but Black women have peeped that, despite all our posturing and protestations, Black men are impotent males unable to perform (dominate) in a social sense.

This leaves us literally up against the wall, especially in the absence of any other operant and respected definition of manhood. To the right is the system defining the man as the dominant creature, to the left is the feminist movement defining the dominant male as the enemy, and in the middle are Black men: dominated by the White man and disrespected by "our women." Oh, how cruel!

WHEN MALES ARE NOT MEN

I think what hurts many of us more than anything about the criticism leveled at us by Black women is not the rightness or the wrongness of the criticism, but the feeling of being swiftly kicked in the groin while we are down. If we were kicking the White man's ass, we would care less. If, indeed, we had the power to kick ass, we would actually be The Man—the man we have been conditioned by modern American mores to believe that all adult males are or should be—the same man that objective political and economic conditions in modern America prevent us from becoming.

If we actually felt we were men and could prove it through political and economic dominance, then being criticized for being a man would not bother us. What really bothers us is that we "non-men," (at best, "aspirant men"), recognize with shame that it is not really our manhood under attack but our *failed* manhood. This failed manhood we desperately desire to bring to fruition. Yet, we realize it is non-functional. To put it even more bluntly: we really want to fuck somebody, but even when we get somebody in our beds, we cannot get it up.

In this context, the paradox is clarified: it is not the Black man who is under attack, but the Black male who ardently wants to be The Man. The painful realization is that even before we become the men we want to be, we perceive that we are attacked for being what in fact we are not. We hurt precisely because the more women talk about how wrong Black men are, the more they reveal to the world how much we are not men in the White western sense of the word, which is the only living, prosperous and unthreatened concept of manhood that most of us know or recognize.

WHEN THE OPPRESSOR DEFINES WHAT IT MEANS TO BE A MAN, THE OPPRESSED MALE CAN NEVER HOPE TO BE A MAN

Once we have accepted the definition of man as dominator, our fate is sealed; White men will not let us dominate and post-70s Black women will not even let us dream of it.

White males dominate Black males (externally by force and internally by establishing the definitions that we unconsciously adopt and use to judge our own manhood or lack thereof.) Even though the White male dominance of us is actually the cause of our psycho-sexual problem, the Black woman's deflating of our manhood aspirations is the coup de grace from which we cannot recover as long as we accept status quo definitions. Neither the macho posturing of the 70s nor the status quo acceptance of the suit-and-tie 80s offered real alternative definitions of manhood. In both instances, we were unconsciously accepting Euro-centric definitions of what it meant for a male to become a man. Whether denouncing or emulating, the measuring rod remained the White man.

This whole psycho-social quandary of seemingly developing our own definition of manhood while really only exhibiting a conditioned and painfully predictable response to our oppression is so subtly complex and ego-damaging that it is hard for many of us to even perceive or admit the effectiveness of this dynamic in immobilizing us. The external dominance we can easily see and just as easily reject. We label it racism. But the internal dominance is so artfully achieved that we adamantly refuse to recognize that our minds are being dominated. We believe that we are creating our own definitions of manhood, but before we can even read and write (not to mention critically and proactively think for ourselves), our vision of self is contaminated by "dominant-culture" produced images of what a man is and should be.

There is not one African American community in America within which the White power structure's definition of manhood is not propagated, supported, and reinforced daily by print and broadcast media. The ubiquitous liquor and cigarette advertising billboards that dominate the physical ghetto landscape are simply the more flagrant and obvious examples of this phenomenon. And do not forget the "police & thieves," especially the police. Currently, this occupying force includes women (more often than not, White women) who handle young African American males like they were boys. Hence, these White women become more "man" than the subjugated Black males.

Moreover, as Fanon correctly perceived and articulated in *A Dying Colonialism*, within the context of colonialism or external domination, it is impossible to come up with an alternative definition of manhood that does not include the committing of violence. Although it is not necessary for us to dominate Whites or women in order to be men, it is necessary for us to destroy the dominance that Whites have over us. As long as we are dominated, we cannot be men; ending our domination will require violence. Long before Fanon, Frederick Douglass framed the essence of this argument: power concedes nothing without a struggle, it never did, and it never will. Whether the violence be physical, mental, or moral is not the question. There is no way to end domination except by force. Contrary to popular belief, there are no shortcuts to power, no shortcuts to achieving enlightened manhood.

IF THE SLAVE WIELDS THE WHIP, DOES THAT MAKE HIM A MAN?

Too many of us focus our energies on defending ourselves against perceived and/or actual feminist attacks. This focus, which fuels a major portion of the anger expressed by Black male writers, is a mistake. No matter what feminists may say about us, feminists are not the enemy. In fact, they do not even talk as bad about us as do our real oppressors.

Since day one (i.e., Jamestown, 1619), African Americans have suffered and continue to suffer systematic oppression and exploitation. Those who maintain this social system are our enemies, regardless of the fact that they now invite us to participate in the system's maintenance. Yet, we suffer from the Frederick Douglass Syndrome: we fight against slavery, and once slavery is abolished we join the government. But it was not slavery alone that was our problem. Our problem was and remains being captured in a social context within which we have relatively insignificant political and economic power.

The most obvious manifestation of the granting of civil rights to African Americans has been the proliferation of Black (predominantly male) elected officials in general and Black mayors of major American cities specifically. The most obvious manifestation of the denial of Black power has been the worsening conditions of inner-city African Americans. This includes not only a debilitating drug epidemic and horrendous ievels of homelessness, but a family profile that is now dominated by female-headed, single-parent families. On the one hand, "blood" is the mayor. On the other hand, he is the absent father/husband.   The resultant dichotomy understandably leads to many politically active men defending the system and many socially active women attacking that same system.

This does not necessarily translate into an anti-male bias on the part of women, but it does mean that women are less likely to believe that participation in electoral politics will solve our social problems. After all, during a period when we have had more Black elected officials than ever before, the conditions of poor women have drastically deteriorated. No matter if Jesse Jackson is elected president, the United States government and the major corporations ultimately represent enemy forces unless and until objective conditions for our people drastically change in the economic, social, and political spheres. How one perceives the enemy is a litmus test. The Black male writer is intricately involved in this inter-community conflict.

In the 60s, we took on racism. In the 90s, we must take on homelessness, drugs, cancer, AIDS, environmental poisoning, economic exploitation, and public (mis)education.   Even though Black men direct many of the local, state, and federal agencies responsible for dealing with these issues, is there any doubt that the same system that produced racism produces and/or condones the ills we now face? The symptoms of the illness are different, but the illness is the same. Whereas before it was White mayors siccing dogs and "pigs" (police) on our people, now we have Black mayors, such as Wilson Goode, who are both figuratively and literally dropping bombs on us. Whereas under segregation all-White school boards enforced inferior education, today, majority-Black school boards very often supervise the miseducation of our youth.

In far too many cases, the most conspicuous examples of "Black men" in our contemporary communities are those who are also tacit collaborators in the maintenance of the system of our oppression and exploitation. During slavery, a similar phenomenon did not create similar confusion. A Black overseer wielding the whip did not change the social conditions one iota for the majority of our people. No slave was fooled into thinking that the creation of Black overseers was an objective improvement for the enslaved majority. Everyone knew the Black overseer had cast his lot with the slave master in exchange for personal gain. Was this Black overseer The Man? NO! The Black overseer was a servant at best, a flunky and traitor at worse. What of today's civil servants?

The dilemma facing Black males is that it is difficult to advocate active participation within the system and at the same time attack the system. We know that the system is not working, but as the repression of the 70s and the 80s* has made clear, there is nowhere outside of and in opposition to the system where it is safe and/or comfortable for a Black man to be a man. Participation in the system offers us a limited measure of manhood, but it is a Pyrrhic victory. What profits it a man to win his manhood if the cost is managing the oppression of his people?

Of course, many will argue that Black men working within the system are making a positive difference. My response is that the difference has been insignificant when compared to the worsening of our overall conditions as a people. Whether politicians are making a significant difference or not, what is the overall condition of our people? The answer is obvious: we are in bad shape. To use a voguish phrase which implies an acceptance of economic determinism, *the bottom line* is that

---

*e.g. Cointelpro, the invasion of Grenada, the destabilization of Jamaica.

most visible and "respected" Black men are promoting integration into the American system rather than independent opposition or alternatives to the American system as the direction of the future.

Among the integrationists, those of us who are Black male writers find ourselves increasingly confounded with nothing original to say. We are confounded because the major issues facing our people all involve opposing the status quo, and how do you be in and out at the same time? We have nothing original to say because there is nothing original about "selling out." Excuse me, there is nothing original about doing what you got to do to deal with the bottom line. Po' boy did it to himself. Our silence on the major issues of the day is a result of our correct understanding that the system does not want to address these issues (from a radical as opposed to an accommodationist perspective). To take a hard line against the system would be a case of biting the hand that feeds us.

Black writers must make the choice that Paul Robeson identified: the choice between the forces of oppression and the forces of freedom. Regardless of rhetoric emanating from Black politicians and Black conservatives, the status quo does not represent freedom for the majority of African Americans. The ethical question each writer faces is not a question of what political line to espouse, but rather how to resolve the conflict between the good of the individual and the good of the group within the context of modern American society. This question is especially critical when we are specifically dealing with the good of our people as a whole versus our own individual economic well-being. The complexities of these questions are the central tension that either activates or paralyzes many Black male writers. The abstract resolution of this conflict is easy:

Revolution against the system and/or significant change within the system.   But on a day-to-day living level, the concrete resolution is not only far more complex, it is also depressing. The inability to make revolution silences us.

For those of us who remain constant in our opposition to the system, we often end up marginalized into a position of very limited, if any, effectiveness. Not surprisingly, we are demoralized by our own ineffectiveness. The media spotlight (the major validator of any reality in contemporary America) focuses on those who participate and excel at partisan politics, while our own fractured, crippled, and largely deserted or nonexistent revolutionary (or alternative) organizations are largely ignored. Those who keep the faith generally find themselves in economically untenable and unenviable positions. There is a whole lot of isolation and very little reward or recognition given to those who oppose the system.

For those of us who try to change the system from the inside, we too end up marginalized. We strive mightily, but even as we are successful at making little changes for the better, the overall position of our people worsens. Most Black male writers who work inside the system in economically secure positions find their creative output drops to a trickle. This happens not because anyone is telling them not to write, nor because someone is telling them what not to write, but because we are not ready—for reasons as understandable as seeing the kids through school to reasons as personal as being tired of being poor, marginalized, and part of an opposition that has proven ineffective at bringing about revolution—to write our most relevant missive: our letter of resignation from the system.

Because of the lack of progress for the majority of our people in all of the places where there have been real revolu-

tions—the failure of Marxist-Leninism and Maoism, the neoco-
lonial embarrassments on the continent of Africa and in the
Caribbean, the crippled Central American revolutions, and the
repressed South American revolutions—one almost feels like a
fool calling for revolution, especially when one has a job in
which one can do small bits of good on a daily basis. Many of
us are emotionally whipped and overcome by the American
political success at counter-revolution. And rather than address
the depth of our pain, the real causes of our impotence, rather
than write about ourselves as we actually are, we suffer in
silence. Meanwhile, the dominant forces march on and on, and
right on over us.

I know from personal experience working as the executive director of the New Orleans Jazz & Heritage Foundation
from June 1983 through June 1987 that no matter how successful a Black person is while working within the system, his or her
success does nothing to answer our people's need for radical,
systematic change. When one honestly realizes the depth of the
dilemma, one either gets out or becomes a silent cynic. We
become silent because we cannot afford to say anything
contrary to the master who employs us or to the field slaves who
see us as house servants. We become cynical because we
realize that the better we do our jobs, the more difficult it will
be to overthrow the system.

READ OUR TRICKS

Jazz musician Archie Shepp is credited with a witty, albeit
deadly accurate, statement: "When we ain't got much, we
share. When we get something, we talk share." As I remember
it, he was discussing the dying out of collectives among jazz
musician, and the absence of any Black collectively owned

record labels.   Writers, more so than most other artists, are magnificent rationalizers. But no amount of rationalization can justify African American abdication of the struggle for independent (or "alternative") publishing apparatuses. The reasons the existing Black presses continue to struggle for recognition is not because they are not taking care of business, nor because they are not publishing important books, but because all of us collectively and most of us individually have failed to financially support their efforts or to establish the necessary support networks, such as distribution companies.

Brothers, Black male writers, we can talk trash if we want to and cry crocodile tears about our plight, but the fact is we just are not doing it. Although the reasons we do not have more healthy, independent, Black publishing businesses is complex, two easily identifiable factors significantly contribute to our failure:

1.   Many of the most financially stable of us have gone the accommodationist route and spent our resources supporting and touting Black-oriented publishing concerns that are either mainstream institution-supported (Black oriented but supported by dominant-culture educational and philanthropic institutions) or they are mainstream aspirant (Black-oriented but they view Blackness as simply a marketing segment or orientation). There is a world of difference between being Black-oriented and being an independent, self-defined, self-determined Black institution.

2.   During the big debate of the late 70s (Black Nationalism vs. Marxism) the progressive wing fractured, and Black Nationalism got a bad rep. Although there were some very important and accurate criticisms leveled against

Black Nationalism, the African American Nationalist community was at the front line of independent and alternative Black institutional development. Black Marxists made two fundamental critiques. First, they denounced the preoccupations of mainstream-aspirant Black business people as the pipe dreams of capitalists who were simply and solely interested in making money. Secondly, the Marxists took a hard-line ideological position that it was impossible to build economic alternatives inside capitalist America. The mainstream-aspirant Black capitalists ignored the Marxists and took shelter in minority set-aside programs and economic schemes concocted by Black politicians. The Nationalists, from whose ranks many of the hard-line Black Marxists emerged, suffered both from the defections and from the fierce and debilitating battle royales that accompanied the transformations of individuals and organizations from Nationalism to staunch Marxists. By the end of the 80s, on the international scene as well as within the United States' African American community, it was clear that both the Marxists and the Nationalists were largely defeated in their quests to establish alternatives. Much of the non-progressive Black business community went rightward with Reagan and the Nationalists were hounded into obscurity. Ironically, the progressive Marxists were often the ones who served as the "hunting dogs" that flushed the Nationalists out of the community.

Historically Black colleges, as well as Black Studies departments and courses at most U.S. colleges and universities, continue to exist. Black professors and Black administrators in these educational institutions could have organized themselves to support ten or fifteen medium-sized presses (those with gross annual sales exceeding a million dollars). Yet, only a small percentage of the books purchased and used in these academic settings are published by independent African American businesses. That is our fault.

The continued existence, growth and development of various Black publishers, such as Africa World Press, Black Classic Press, Third World Press, and others is the major exception to the just outlined depressing scenario.   Their existence demonstrates that it can be done. Yet much remains to be done. Dealing with self-capitalization is where there is an understandably significant difference between the independent Black movement and the women's movement. The women's movement receives major and consistent capitalization from women who have access to money, an access that easily outweighs any comparison of access to wealth in the Black community.

There are more than enough Black male writers who are employed as professors and endowed with prestigious fellowships and grants to fund a national Black literary publication, if not a Black publishing company. Besides our own hesitancy to leave the big house (where we are seduced and corrupted by creature comforts), what stops us? When we did not have access to the resources, we used to try to build independent publishing concerns. Now that a significant number of Black male writers are employed and have access (at the very least) to personal resources we talk about the silencing of the Black male writer. Brothers, please!

In the area of literary magazines, the two major independently produced, nationally distributed Black literary magazines, *Catalyst* and *Shooting Star Review* are both founded and edited by African American women—Pearl Cleage and Sandra Gould Ford, respectively. *Catalyst* is funded by the Fulton County (GA) Arts Council and *Shooting Star* is far from being really well known around the country. Regardless of these shortcomings, where Black (mainly male) politicians have risen to nominal positions of power or influence, we do not use our power or influence to create and support independent Black publishing efforts. Fellows, where are we?

Journals such as *Obsidian* and *Callaloo* can be cited as publications founded and edited by Black male writers, but both are connected to universities, and both actually underscore the point that we men are not out on the cutting edge of alternative magazine publishing. It is not that Black men are not doing anything, nor that what we do is not of merit. Yet, African American male writers have all but abandoned the struggle to create independent Black publishing institutions.

Women are much clearer about both the necessity of self-determination and about making a personal commitment to establishing independent publishing concerns. While most Black male writers are writing for status quo-based publications, women are breaking down the barriers as well as creating their own women-controlled publishing institutions.

Black male writers are not so much silent as we are generally irrelevant in the struggle to create an alternative to the status quo. We think progressive thoughts, but our actions and inactions suggest we have abdicated a leadership position in our liberation struggle. To paraphrase Stevie Wonder, it is not that we are silent, but when we talk, "we ain't saying nothing."

BACK TO THE BUSH

Brothers, if you're still with me, let's do like Isaac Hayes advises and make a big fat "U-Turn." Our real problem is not silence. The real question is: will we continue talking loud and saying nothing or will we add our voices in shouting a freedom song? We know what the real deal is. Our impotence is self-inflicted and based on our decision to stand in the shadow of the master. The revivification of our virility is directly related to our willingness to speak out, and act out, against oppression and exploitation.

If we are convinced that we are headed in the right direction, then so be it. But in the process of silently giving assent to the slaughter, let's not blame anyone but ourselves. If we have been silenced, it is because of our own overwhelming feelings of inadequacy and guilt. As Black male writers, we silenced ourselves once we stopped struggling for freedom from the system and convinced ourselves that collaboration and accommodation was the prudent course! WORD!

Sun Song IX

*sometimes i think i have not done enough
to make the world safe for love*
(a letter to Linda/i waz just thinking)

*safe for dreams, safe for children, for unfenced flower
gardens and for lonely late night walks just because
at two a.m. on any given night you want to walk and
think, and think and walk, alone, down some street, near or
far from home, and safe for visa-unnecessary visits from world
lovers and comrades, from dignitaries and unknowns from
nations whose names we can't spell, safe for teen-agers
to have slumber parties unchaperoned and sleep seven
on the floor with the front door forgotten
unlocked, for medical care always available
for a baby coughing at midnight almost choking
and unable to sleep and parents unable to sleep
and no money necessary to get this child treated, for
world cinema shown at the corner show, for 24-hour jazz
radio and reggae radio, and opera and blues day
blues night, for celebratory tangos and drum choirs from
ghana and television shows of poets reading, safe for
committed literature uncensored, printed in popular
editions and sold for a quarter or so at the
local newsstand, every local newsstand, in every
country, in every language that's readable,
literature as abundant as guns and bombs are today, like
that, right next to fruit and vegetables, on top
of the counters of corner stalls, safe for*

not having to flinch when a police siren screams
or even when three or more policemen come walking toward
me, safe for an end to world leaders whose average age,
    temperament
and physical condition makes it impossible for them to dance
or giggle, for an end to bad drinking water and unending
nuclear waste, the threat of misinformation shrouded covert
operations, for the immediate cessation of the strategic blowing
of natural resources into space while urban-scapes
rot and become the dumping grounds for tons of non
bio-degradable trash, safe for honoring human beings with deeds
rather than cement statues with swords, rifles and flags
unpraised, for memorializing strugglers who have made a positive
difference by erecting libraries and cultural centers, hospitals
and bus stations named for them, safe for writing
to overseas friends and the postage rate lowered
for personal letters & picture post cards & cassettes,
safe for big black multi-ton whales to warble sub water and frolic
sticking their tails out of the sea as they dive up and down,
safe for the mental health of everyone and the housing
of the man who smells (his skin patina so weathered you can
not tell if he is black or white) sleeping on the steps of
some towering stone building in six layers of oversized
clothes dirty as the metropolitan sidewalk his head resting
in pigeon shit, for an end to looking at each other crooked,
influenced by some foolishness, we don't know where
it comes from, me sitting in my skin castle with racial
rooms that have one little window and a locked door, sitting
behind thick, class-erected walls breathing stale air, squatting
in my gender fortress, and you just as vigilant holed-up
in yours, several moats of bad feelings and misunderstandings
separating us, safe for talking eye to eye instead of
communicating with hastily scribbled messages tied
to rocks that we bizarrely heave between us-selves,

back and forth, under the misleading title of official
government communiques, safe for an unconditional & immu-
>*table*
world law which prohibits soldiers leaving the places
wherever they were born, for a 365-day a year amusement
park where we can send old war lords, ex-presidents, premieres
& prime ministers and all others who think they are qualified
to run, rule and ruin the world so they can play
games to their hearts' content and not hurt themselves nor
us, safe for smiles and honestly talking to people we've never
met before, for riding a bust home after midnight without
a gun, safe even for snakes to cross a road without
somebody's self-righteous boot-heel crushing their heads simply
because they're a different kind of animal,
safe for artistic expression and yes, safe and sometimes also, really
safe all the time also, for silly expressions, and gentle
laughter as well as safe too for those screamers
that make your side hurt when your friends mimic the way you bug
your eyes when you are angry or the way i rub my jaw when
i am embarrassed, and we be walking down the street some spring
day eating hot apple pie licking our fingers on the way to tutor
and play ball with some kids somewhere, or is it the Black
Women's International Photo Exhibit called "Soul Eyes" that we
are going to, sometimes i know i haven't done enough
to make the world safe for love — i promise to do better

Why I Read Out/Look

A good friend asked me the other day "why are you reading *that*"? She was referring to *Out/Look*, a nationally circulated gay quarterly. My answer was immediate, "because I'm interested in the human experience. I want to know and understand as much as I can."

I did not talk about the politics of supporting gay rights or the importance of taking what I considered to be a progressive stand on the question of human sexuality. Nor did I jump to the offensive and ask: "Why even ask? Don't you support gay rights?"

While it would be easy to be self-congratulatory about my open mindedness on the gay issue, it would be false. Just as individuals who take pride in not being a racist but who do not actively engage in fighting against racism, we must move beyond what we think and begin the task of changing the social order which invariably will require challenging and changing the way a significant number of people think and act. Although I am unapologetic in my focus on freedom for people of African descent, I do not believe that this struggle means freedom only for us.

When we are fighting racism, sexism, or whatever, it is easy to define our struggle as a fight against a specific enemy.

If we are not careful, the devil becomes more important than the struggle as a whole. We end up loosing sight of the core reason for struggle: our struggle is a struggle to create a world where *all* human beings can live free of social oppression and exploitation.

In our case, we can not afford to define our struggle narrowly as a struggle against White supremacy. If we do, we become confused by neo-colonialism, we balk at supporting struggles by people of European descent, we are unable to make the connection between our struggle and sexism, and on the issue of gay rights specifically, we refuse to have dialogue around the issues at all.

I am sometimes surprised by the depth of homophobia among many of our people who claim or appear to be progressive. Historically, there have always been visible gays in African American communities—from the female impersonators and flamboyant show business personalities, many of whom were well known among those who lived or enjoyed the night life in urban centers across this country, to the barely concealed and tacitly accepted (albeit "officially" denounced) church subculture of homosexual male gospel singers. Given the pervasiveness of homosexuality in our communities, one would think that there would be, if not a championing of gay rights, at least a tolerance. However, that is not the case.

Undoubtedly, the AIDS scare has had a lot to do with a surge in homophobia. But AIDS hysteria does not fully explains this current wave of homophobia. Many of us are simply uncomfortable with the mere thought of homosexuality. This discomfort reflects our lack of comfort with our own marginality. When one is secure about one's identity, people with a different identity are not perceived as threats nor as deformed. But as our preoccupation with hair and cosmetics indicate, African Americans as a people are still unsure about who and what we want to be and how we identify our humanity.

Out-of-the-closet gays and lesbians agitating for their human rights challenge us to define humanity as larger than ourselves and larger than our mythical-macho image of our oppressors (mythical because many of their cultural heroes are gay). Self-assertive homosexuals also challenge us to recognize as human specific modes of sexual behavior that we have been reared to think of as repulsive, sinful and/or deviant.

We are often uncomfortable with gays precisely because the gay lifestyle challenges us to expand our definition of what is acceptable human behavior. Our failure to support gay rights is not because gays are physically attacking us, ridiculing us in the media, nor making fun of us on the streets. We avoid gays because they challenge us to expand our concept of what it means to be human.

Gays make us uncomfortable with the way we are. And to the degree that we are uncomfortable with the mere existence of a group of people who have never collectively done us any harm, we demonstrate how uncomfortable we are with ourselves. Contact with gays or being confronted by manifestations of gay lifestyles in print, film or music force us to either accept or reject that lifestyle, *those* people. That choosing is in fact also a process of defining humanity.

Either we believe gays are despicable and worthy of contempt or else we believe they are unfairly discriminated against and the struggle for their rights should be supported. The "I'm not for them or against them" argument holds no water when people are being discriminated against, physically attacked, and made the butt of offensive jokes and media representations. Just as the struggle against segregation forced everyone to choose sides, the struggle for gay rights does the same.

Shamefully, many of us are so turned off by what we perceive as a "repugnant" sexual lifestyle, we find no way to actively raise our voices, not to mention become actively involved in struggles for gay rights. Worse yet, some of us refuse to accept the gay lifestyle as a valid part of the human experience. For some of us (indeed, for too many of us), gays are pathological. This leads many of us who are not otherwise very religious to quote the *Bible*, the *Torah*, or the *Koran*, suggesting that our creator has ordained gays as unnatural and sinful.

The other frequently cited argument against gays is that we must protect our children from the influence of gays (and here we usually lower our voices as though sharing some state secret that verges on breaching so-called national security). Others insist we must protect our children from sexual abuse by gays, totally ignoring the numerous studies which make clear that very few of the perpetrators are out of the closet gays. The majority of child abusers actually are heterosexual or bisexual males. Although a significant number of us may actually believe otherwise, the truth is, closeted Catholic priests and closeted Baptist gospel singers are a bigger threat to homosexuality influencing our children than are out of the closet gays. And, in case the reference to "Catholic priests" and "Baptist gospel singers" is a bit too subtle, I am simply putting up-front and in print what many of us whisper about day in and day out. There is a large degree of covert homosexual activity in the religious community. It is the "covertness" of such activity that often makes our opposition to gays hard to deal with because covertness by definition also includes concealment and denial of the activity's existence by those who participate in and/or condone the behavior.

Pedophilia is a red herring used to mask our own confusion about how to relate to people who are just like us except for their perceived sexually abnormality. What makes us uncomfortable is not that homosexuals threaten our connection to the creator, or that they are an actual threat to our children. Rather, we are uncomfortable with the reality that homosexuals seem to be so much like us and, at the same time, we perceive them to be sexually, repulsively different.

Homosexuality repulses many of us partly because we are afraid that we ourselves harbor latent tendencies. Worse yet, we fear being forced or seduced into committing the unspeakable crime: a homosexual sexual act. Although we vehemently reject such *personal defilement*, we are simultaneously fixated on paying an inordinate amount of attention to that which we say we are not interested in.

Why does the mere presence of a homosexual threaten our emotional stability? Could it be that we are not as sexually stable as we try to convince ourselves we are?

I support human rights for all people regardless of their specific identity. Does this mean I support human rights for White people and gays? Yes, unequivocally yes!

Everyone has the right to life. And it is our responsibility to fight for the human rights of every human being, especially those who are victims within the same social system that oppresses and exploits us.

Life is a spectrum. We cannot remain focused on one sector of that spectrum. Those of us who have no interest in learning about others and choose to avoid the so-called difficult questions about the nature of humanity will find that ignoring or denying the humanity of those we do not understand or accept inevitably leads to us limiting our own selves.

While those who are in power aggrandize material gains through oppression and exploitation, we, the marginals, the alienated, the oppressed and exploited gain nothing—except perhaps a prolonging of our own dis-empowerment—by being narrow-minded and contemptuous of each other because we are different. We have no excuse for mimicking the attitudes and actions of those whom we say we want to overthrow.

Both the long and short of it is simple: I read *Out/Look* because knowledge is healthier than ignorance, humanity is broader than any one individual lifestyle, I have brothers and sisters who are gays and lesbians—and though I am different from them, it is a difference of degree and not of kind. We are all human beings. All of us.

II.

While I consider my politics ethically correct, my self perceived political correctness does not totally explain why I read *Out/Look*. I do not read *Out/Look* simply because the journal's perspective is "correct" or even because I am "correct." I also read *Out/Look* because it is a professionally produced and intellectually engaging magazine that attractively presents a broad range of information I want to read. It is not simply the politics.

There are a number of magazines that publish information I am interested in or that I share a political line with. I do not read most of them on a regular basis generally because most of them are dull, deadly boring periodicals.

For me, reading *Out/Look* is not simply based upon a

political position. The truth is I do not regularly read any other gay/lesbian periodicals. We accept comrades based on commonality in struggle, we choose friends and lovers based on compatibility, desire (they make us "feel good"), and self esteem (they make us "feel special"). Of course, it is best when our friends and lovers are also our comrades, but that is not always the case. I regard *Out/Look* as both comrade and friend.

On the design level, there are few magazines, and especially few politically oriented magazines that are as attractively designed. *Out/Look* is attractive without being slick, trendy or pop-modern. Each article has its own unique layout and the production team utilizes a wide range of artists and photographers. The type size is large. Rather than jamming as much as possible on each page, *Out/Look* utilizes an aesthetically pleasing balance of white space, art, and copy.

Editorially, this is by far one of the best edited magazines on the general market. After 13 years as an editor of the *Black Collegian* magazine, I know the difficulties of editing a periodical. *Out/Look* is consistently engaging and each issue features a wide range of ideas and/or sharing of viewpoints. There is a good mix of factual reporting, opinion pieces, polemics, and creative writing without one bit of pandering to a "cross over" audience. This is the way special interest publishing should be done if it is to be effective. There is a lesson here. If African American activists are to successfully organize our people, as well as build supportive coalitions with other peoples and other interest groups, then it is necessary that we develop organs which honestly and successfully argue our case. Two African American journals of the recent past exemplified this same approach, *The Liberator* (edited by Dan Watts) and *Negro Digest/Black World* (edited by Hoyt Fuller). Both publications exemplified the attractively packaged, editorially broad periodical that is needed to inform and inspire a movement. *Out/ Look* is a good contemporary model and this concept is crying out for continuance.

III.

I read an article in *Out/Look* on language which proposes a shift from the term homophobia to heterosexism. The point is to shift the weight from a focus on homosexuals to a focus on the sexism of heterosexuals. It is an important distinction and offers a solid contribution to the use of language, especially the process of defining, as a tool of struggle.

I first encountered the term "heterosexism" in the work of Audre Lorde, an African American lesbian writer and one of the strongest writers of the modern era. She is a world force in terms of her ability to speak to issues, clarify contradictions and challenge accepted ideas. She is especially fearless in proposing the creative use of anger and voice among and by those who often suffer silently. When I read the essay, I immediately thought of Audre Lorde and wondered if she had been an inspiration for this author.

The cogent essay delved into the psychology of heterosexism vs. homophobia and offered more than simply a rationale for the use of one and the discarding of the other. The essay also was an inspirational example of self-definition in the face of oppression.

My immediate point of reference is of course our struggle in the 60s to move from Negro to Black (& African, or African American / Afro-American). We fought hard on that one and won. Although from where we are today it may not seem like much of a victory, any time we can successfully wage a struggle over definition, over acceptance of our own self definition as opposed to the definition offered by our oppressor, than we have indeed waged and won a valuable struggle.

Clearly, this essay convinced me to adopt the term heterosexism and, for general use, discard homophobia. Enough said.

IV.

In response to those who think we are divided enough without having to deal with the "divisive" question of homosexuality, I respond who's doing the dividing. I am calling for unity, sharing, enlargement of the community rather than the excommunication of those who we think of as different or even deviant. Moreover, whether we like them or not, find them attractive or repulsive, these are our children, brothers and sisters, parents, aunts and uncles, ancestors, and destiny. They are as much a part of us as we are a part of them. As much as they have been rejected and alienated from us, we have been rejected and alienated from ourselves.

Homosexuals are generally despised and especially rejected by many politically active folk, but that is a weakness on our part. We are wrong to buy into prejudice and chauvinism. I remember back in the early 80s, when we at Ahidiana began to articulate and act on our opposition to sexism, we caught some flack but we also opened some eyes. There were some who vehemently expressed their concern and opposition when we invited a known lesbian to speak as a Black lesbian on a panel at one of the Black Woman's Conferences. Some people in the community thought we had lost our minds. Indeed, within our organization, some strong struggle went down before we publicly took our position. Just as waging that struggle strengthened rather than weakened us, fighting both sexism and heterosexism will strengthen rather than weaken our organizations.

Many gays and lesbians have been negatively effected by the general positions of many of us in the nationalist community, and a great deal of resentment and ill will persists because of this. Nevertheless, the unifying and healing of our community must begin somewhere. I think it is on us, especially those of us who threw rocks in the past, to extend the olive branch of peace and the helping hand of friendship. We must make homosexuals welcome in our struggle and must extend ourselves to support their specific struggles for acceptance and human rights.

V.

I love James Baldwin.

VI.

There are those who argue that homosexuality is not natural. I understand that homosexuality is not "normal" but I think there is a big difference between not normal and unnatural. Human behavior is a spectrum and the edges are often far from the norm. Homosexuality is far from the norm but it is not unnatural.

Two young men kissing. Openly. On the street. Their tongues down each other's throat. Effeminate mannerisms. The mere thought of four hard legs in bed, not to mention other hard parts. This repulses many of us.

Two sisters kissing. Openly. On the street. Their tongues down each other's throat. Masculine mannerisms. The mere thought of four fine thighs in bed, not to mention other fine parts. This too repulses many of us.

A heterosexual couple kissing. Openly. On the street. Their tongues down each other's throat. Feminine and masculine mannerisms together. The mere thought of this couple in bed, merging into each other. This attracts many of us.

Why? Because the heterosexual is the norm, the average, the median and the homosexual, the extreme, the divergent, the edge. We are comfortable with ourselves and uncomfortable with the other. Yet, sexuality does not rub off.

We argue the Biblical —or other religious—prohibitions. The "them" against "us" dichotomy. Yet, if we truthfully read our traditional societies, we find there is a wider acceptance of human nature than there is in so-called modern, sophisticated society. Worldwide, we find traditional societies were often stratified in terms of the social functions of gender and homosexuals were stratified into gender based social functions. Yet, such stratification did not include condemnation as an abomination.

Both the relatively "new" religions of Christianity and Islam intersect in their rejection of homosexuality. These religions are "new" in the context of human history. These new religions are not the best starting points for a discussion of what is "normal" because humans have lived for thousands of years before the founding of these two religions. Therefore, these religions may be "abnormal" rather than the other way around. Perhaps within the context of human history, the acceptance of homosexuality may be the norm of progressive societies rather than what we hold as the norm today. Regardless of the past, acceptance of the variety of human sexual expression is preferable to the repression of mutually consensual sexual expression between adults. (However a given society may define adults.) Acceptance of life, in all its variety, is what is truly sane and normal.

I do not want to live nor love in a society that is narrowly normal. I do not want to see a rainbow with just one color. I do not need agreement to be comfortable. What we need more than agreement is honesty and openness.

Sun Song X

the murder of amilcar cabral

be careful what evils you tolerate
or how easily you blink away the blood of others
as though murder were simply water under the bridge

be careful, look beyond appearances
to the blind, dead fish and jelly roll funk smell the same
there should be an amber light in both your nostrils

read the fine print, don't just sign your name
to unexamined copy, your x on this earth spot
will be used one day to demonstrate that you complied
remember, every vote is a wrong vote
if you have only voted for the lesser
of what you did not want to vote for in the first place

don't claim ignorance, ignorance of reality is no excuse
a little steam of sweetening can make atrocities
palatable if you just want the illusion of health
why does a dead animal, a decapitated chicken for instance
or a angus bull whose throat has been slit, seem
to smell better after it has been cooked,
is it not still dead and decaying?

listen closely to everything that is not man made
for instance, the trees crying

their tears of acid rain scarring their tender
brittle barks as branches are cut off to make
toilet paper, ah i envy the bears who shit in the woods
at least they have cut out the charmin' middle men profiteering
off our need to cleanse our funky behinds

remember, nothing that is absolute is relevant
relativity rules us all
bach will be bach will be bach regardless of where he's played
but there can be no secondline without dancers

there is danger in reading without thinking
why are we taught to read but not to think, there
is danger, like the times picayune,
a paper in which it takes longer to read the ads
than to read the articles, early in this century
the picayune in typically backward prophesy warned us
about the addictive evils of jazz but it was too late
to save the symphony that spends millions of dollars each
year and has yet to produce a pops, a jelly roll or
anyone who has changed the way the world hears music
some of you will not understand this poem, that's alright
it took me a long time to understand that the murder
of amilcar cabral was just a dress rehearsal for
the inner-city slaughter of our youth confronted
by their own ignorance of who and what the real enemy is

be careful, dear hearts, be careful
the present is not a safe place to sleep

The Failure of Integration
Where We Been &
How We Got The Way We Are

In the face of a near-total collapse of African American community life and an alarming increase of racially motivated attacks throughout the country, political pundits and others are beginning to question the wisdom of integration—traditionally defined as the merging of African Americans into the American mainstream. As Salim Muwakkil declares, "Increasing numbers of analysts—both black and white—are blaming many social ills on past strategies that placed too much focus on the need for full racial integration."[1] Muwakkil goes on to note that Benjamin Hooks, former executive director of the NAACP (National Association for the Advancement of Colored People), takes the position that "much of what needs to be done within the African-American community must be done by ourselves and for ourselves."[2]

This is a reversal of historic proportions. As Harold Cruse astutely delineates, "the term 'integration' as NAACP social policy appears in 1940 in response to the government's Selective Service Act"[3] when the U.S. was preparing to enter World War II. Cruse meticulously outlines the development of

---

1. "Black Leaders Favor 'Self-help' over Integration," *In These Times* (Oct. 10-16, 1990).
2. Ibid.
3. "The Past and Future of Integration," *Sojourners* (August-September 1990).

integration as a NAACP policy and perceptively notes that NAACP calls for integration of the armed forces during WWII were ignored. Integration of the military, which remains the most integrated sector of American society, was first actualized during the Korean conflict.* At that time, "unlike previous wars, the United States was fighting a non-white nation and had no 'racial' qualms about using blacks liberally as infantry."[4]

Beginning with the famous 1954 *Brown* decision outlawing "separate but equal" schools, the civil rights struggle entered a mass movement phase that quickly outstripped the "litigation movement" phase chiefly advocated by the NAACP. While some argue that the civil rights movement was an integrationist movement, it is more accurately analyzed as a desegregationist movement—that is, a movement to end the legal obstruction of African American access to participation in public life. As Manning Marable writes,

> The leaders of the desegregation social protest movement a generation ago mobilized millions with one simple demand—"freedom." In the context of the "Jim Crow" or racially segregated society of the South in the post-World War II period, freedom meant the elimination of all social, political, legal, and economic barriers that forced black Americans into a subordinate status.[5]

Following the 1954-1964 decade of struggle, the desegregation movement disintegrated, paradoxically and precisely because it achieved its victory with the passage of the 1964 civil rights and 1965 voting rights legislation. After that, the question

---

* A logical extension of integration of the armed forces during the Korean conflict was fueled in part by the activism of returning vets who often fought many small battles at home to maintain the level of access to the mainstream that integration offered within the armed services.

4. Ibid.

5. "What's Wrong with Integration?," *Sojourners* (August-September 1990).

was no longer "freedom" (then popularly defined as desegregation), but rather, as poignantly posed by Dr. Martin Luther King, Jr., "Where do we go from here?"

In 1966 during the March Against Fear in Mississippi, SNCC (Student Nonviolent Coordinating Committee) organizers Kwame Ture (Stokeley Carmichael) and Willie Ricks gave militant voice to the slogan, "Black Power." The struggle for ideological hegemony and political direction of the former civil rights movement was on.

By 1968, with the assassination of Dr. King, the national uproar over the Viet Nam War, and the concomitant mainstream social destabilization created by movements such as Women's Rights and Gay Rights, integration became a major social policy question for the whole nation. The challenge posed to the U.S. by former civil rights activists was magnified by a larger nationwide struggle that White activists waged against the status quo. During the late 60s and early 70s, many of these antiwar, feminists and other activists received their political baptism in the rivers of fire of the civil rights movement. All of America stood at the crossroads waging a convulsive and sometimes violent struggle over social direction and national policy.

At this point, a confluence of social forces led to "integration" becoming more than simply a litigation tactic for minority rights and more than a synonym for desegregation. The American body politic consciously decided to either pursue or push "integration" (depending on whether it was the majority or minority communities in motion) as a social policy. This historic moment was vulgarly crystallized when President Johnson, a true "good ole boy," joined the chorus with a straight face to sing "We Shall Overcome." This anthem of the desegregation civil rights movement was stood on its head by a Dixiecrat who decided it was politically easier to co-opt the desegregation movement under the rubric of "integration" than to oppose desegregation.

In response to King's question, "where do we go from here," the various factions within the African American community coalesced into two main groupings: the integrationists and the Black Nationalists. In terms of ideology, organizational style, programs, tactics, and stated goals, the contending forces had little in common and often were directly at odds with each other.

Integration was championed by what became known as the moderates, or the old guard—the NAACP, SCLC (Southern Christian Leadership Council), some factions of CORE (Congress of Racial Equality), and the lesser recognized but extremely important nexus of African American church organizations: the Southern Baptist Association. The leadership of integration was personified by Dr. King. The overall thrust of this movement was characterized as a southern-based and rural effort by Blacks to be one with Whites.

SNCC brought national attention to the Black Power movement. This movement quickly mushroomed, and various branches of Black Nationalism (between 1965 and 1975) became the dominant ideology of the masses of African Americans. Variations of Black Power often widely divergent and sometimes even at odds with each other were championed by organizations such as the racially reformed (Whites were dismissed) SNCC, the resurgent Nation of Islam headed by the Honorable Elijah Muhammad, the newly organized Black Panther Party, the armed movement for reparations spearheaded by The Republic of New Afrika, the ideologically potent Los Angeles-based US organization headed by Maulana

Karenga, and its east, coast ideological analogue, The Congress of Afrikan People headed by Amiri Baraka. Additionally, there existed a host of related organizations, all of which worked under the rubric of self-determination and self-defense for the "Black Nation." The fact that many of these organizations were largely unknown to mainstream America in no way diminished the widespread support and impact these organizations had among African Americans. The leadership of Black Nationalism was personified by El Hajj Malik El Shabazz (Malcolm X). The overall thrust of this movement was characterized as an urban-based movement for political and economic power based on community control.

None of the contending forces had a time-tested blueprint, and all of the forces recognized that this was a critical historical moment that offered immediate possibilities for action. Mass demonstrations and rallies were almost a sine qua non of movement activities. These were heady days. Each dawn brought new possibilities as well as new problems; a sense of urgency surrounded every effort.

Given (1) the competition for the allegiance and support of the masses of African Americans, (2) the paucity of material and financial resources within the African American community, and (3) the limited and often programmatically restrictive resources offered by philanthropic and governmental organizations, a great deal of infighting went on within what was then being called the Black Liberation movement. A great deal of external manipulation accompanied this fissure.

Although he overlooks the active participation of the government as the most decisive force, Gary Peller persuasively identifies the nongovernmental forces that coalesced around and pushed for integration. Peller suggests the following as their motivation:

> The transformation of American apartheid could have taken many forms, and even the program of racial integration could have been understood in different ways. But I believe that the universalist character of integrationist ideology satisfied an unstated need to justify the rejection of Black nationalists. This particular ideology of race was not simply "chosen" because it meshed well with traditional liberal ideas about epistemology, historical progress, or social justice. It was constructed in this way in response to the psycho-cultural anxieties about group- and self-identity that Black middle-class moderates and white upper- and middle-class liberals and progressives, and in particular secular Jews, experienced in the face of a revitalized Black nationalist tradition. The myth of universalism helped resolve these anxieties at the ideological level.[6]

Federal government mandates and broad philanthropic and organizational support of integration, as well as the concurrent shunning of Black Nationalism by White liberals and progressives, secured integration as national policy. Yet, had there been a plebiscite among African Americans in the late 60s or early 70s with a choice between integration or nationalism, the majority of African Americans undoubtedly would have voted for nationalism. The desire for Black political and economic power was boldly evident. African Americans were saying it loud: we were "Black and Proud," and we were clear that it was indeed "Nation Time!"

This was when the federal government kicked integration into high gear. This was the crossroads; when Black Nationalist efforts at community control of schools, self-help initiatives such as the Panther's "Free Breakfast" program, and calls for radical revamping of higher education (which precipitated the Black

---

6. *Tikkun* (Vol. 6, No. 1).

Studies movement) were co-opted. Simultaneously, Black Nationalist organizations were systematically repressed, especially under the infamous FBI enacted COINTELPRO domestic counterinsurgency program.

Federal government co-optation took various forms such as Head Start and other so-called anti-poverty program initiatives, "food stamps," and the like. Further, there was the great dividing line of affirmative action, patterned on the United States' treatment of Native Americans: first the government gave its word and made it the law of the land, and then reneged on legislation which they had initiated.

From Johnson to Reagan, government-led integration has been a typically American exercise in government duplicity. The end result of this effort was the de facto legitimation of the destruction of African American communities, allegedly in the pursuit of freedom, democracy, "liberty and justice for all." While the popular misconception is that integration was what Blacks were clamoring for, the views and well-being of African Americans were not the actual defining factor in these government programs. The substance of integration consisted of federal and state guidelines promulgated by a corps of bureaucrats, most of whom, along with their conservative corporate counterparts, were holdovers from the previous segregationist regimes of federal and state government.

As Peller correctly points out:

> ...many of the same whites who once carried out the program of American apartheid actually kept their jobs as the decision-makers in the employment offices of companies and in the admissions offices of schools. In institution after institution, progressive reformers found themselves struggling over the implementation of racial integration with the former administrators of segrega-

tion, who soon regrouped as an old guard "concerned"
over the deterioration of "standards."[7]

Clearly, the dominant White power structure was ipso facto
defining what integration meant in ideological terms and how
it was to be implemented in day-to-day life. Looking back over
what has been done under the rubric of integration, Peller
ruefully concludes:

> In the last three decades, tremendous social resources
> and personal energy have been expended on integrating
> formerly white schools, work places, neighborhoods,
> and attitudes. This program has had some success in
> improving the lives of specific people and in transform-
> ing the climate of overt racial domination that shaped
> American society before the advent of civil rights reform.
> But it has been pursued to the exclusion of a commit-
> ment to the vitality of the Black community as a whole
> and to the economic and cultural health of Black
> neighborhoods, schools, economic enterprises, and indi-
> viduals. It is frustrating to reconsider the long history of
> American race relations from this perspective.[8]

In the terminal decade of the 20th century, both Whites and
African Americans, albeit for different reasons, have come to the
conclusion that integration has failed. As Thomas Byrne Edsall
asserts:

> Significant numbers of white working- and lower-middle-
> class voters—voters essential to a progovernment political
> coalition—perceive civil rights policies as reforms that
> impose taxes on those who work in order to pay the cost
> of services for those who do not. Policies aimed at
> ameliorating the conditions of the poor—focusing on
> matters ranging from welfare regulation to the imple-
> mentation of minority quotas—have contributed to the
> near institutionalization of racial conflict, which also has

---

7. *Tikkun* (Vol. 6, No. 1).
8. Ibid.

> the unwelcome side effect of distorting the economic
> base of national political coalitions.[9]

Social well-being statistics chronicle the obscene reality of what integration has meant for African Americans. By every measure of well-being—income, health, life expectancy, employment, etc.— African Americans are worse off in 1994 than we were a decade ago. It is inaccurate to claim that integration purposefully caused this disintegration of the African American community. However, if the avowed goal of integration was to improve the living conditions of African Americans, integration has failed miserably.

Nathan Glazer responded to Peller with a naiveté that ought to be dismissed as a mean-spirited joke except that Glazer's views mirror the sentiments of many white American decision makers. Glazer innocently asks, "Isn't the election of Black mayors a form of 'transfer of power'? How is that inadequate?"[10] Obviously Glazer has never paused to consider that integrationist "transfer of power," in terms of the election of Black mayors, has not changed the living conditions of the majority of African American residents. In fact, the conditions of cities with Black mayors have deteriorated so drastically that, for the first time in the history of the United States (according to the National Center for Health Statistics), Black life expectancy by 1988 had declined for the past four years. While Black elected officials have been nominally in charge of America's major cities, where over 75% of all African Americans reside, our living conditions have worsened to the point where we (as less than 15% of the general population) have caused a downward turn for the entire country.[11] In that light, how can anyone

---

9. *Tikkun* (Vol. 6, No. 1).
10. Ibid.
11. the *New York Times* (November 29, 1990).

expect African Americans to believe that integration is working?

While it is true that the African American middle class has experienced a significant share of material gain, the cost of the ticket has been ghastly. The gains have come at the sacrifice of self-determined economic structures, the denial of cultural integrity, and the abandonment of political relevance to the overall African American community.

At one time, the African American middle class consisted of entrepreneurs whose clientele was drawn largely from the African American community. The smoke-screen of Black economic gains notwithstanding, the vast majority of today's so-called "Black businesses" of any meaningful size are either franchises of larger corporations, or they are subcontractors supplying major American corporations. These Black businesses are not based on providing goods and services to the African American community, but are actually appendages to the American corporate community. Likewise, they are totally dependent on corporate largesse and noblesse oblige.

Whereas there was a time when aspiring to middle-class status did not mean leaving the community behind, today, riding the integration jet requires one to fly miles above any contact with the masses of African Americans. It is a trip that takes a debilitating psychic toll.

Anthony A. Parker is bitterly on target when he notes:

> ...the practice of integration created the illusion of equality with the wider culture, effectively wresting control of the black freedom movement by holding it hostage to federal good will and weakening or destroying those institutions that influenced blacks' worldview. The effect this loss of control has had on my generation is devastating. Growing up in "integrated" America has established a pattern of cognitive dissonance among young blacks. Inoculated with secular values emphasiz-

> ing the individual instead of the community, and pro-
> gressive politics over theology, young blacks rarely
> recognize each others as brothers and sisters, or as
> comrades in the struggle. We're now competitors, relat-
> ing to each other out of fear and mistrust.[12]

The psychological decimation of Black consciousness is the most debilitating result of integration as practiced in the last half of the 20th century. The most educated and capable among us are also the most brainwashed and psychologically/physically out of touch with the masses of our people. But of course, as our country cousins well knew, once they've seen the bright lights of the big city, it's hard to keep them happy with the lamp lights of the farm.

Yet, who among us does not want to reach the levels of expertise, wealth, education, and leisure that are characteristic of the so-called "American Dream," a dream that literally millions of Whites live every day? We accept integration in pursuit of the American dream, but in the process we ignore the prophetic warnings of James Baldwin against integrating into a burning house.

Baldwin evidenced critical consciousness of both what it means to be an American and Black as well as what it means to have a double identity. Many of us shed this critical consciousness as we rush to dive head-first into the pool of American integration. Rather than change America, we end up becoming apologists for America, often for the worst of what America historically has meant as far as economic and ethical policies are concerned.

Rather than erase the inferiority complex of African Americans, integration has actually reinforced both our feel-

---

12. "Whose America Is It?," Sojouners (August-September 1990).

ings and actualities of inferiority. Moreover, our inferiority complex is no longer simply a self-perception, it is also an ideological predisposition. Today, the majority of us assume that if a venture, organization, or movement is all-Black, then it is inherently remedial (in which case it is temporary), second-rate, or practically and/or ethically wrong. The physical, emotional, or ideological absence of Whites from our dreams and aspirations is psychologically forbidden, unthinkable, and inconceivable—even when we complain about being tired of White people. In a perverse extension of Carter G. Woodson's observation that the miseducated Negro will always seek out a back door and make one where none exists, the integration oriented person of color will always measure her or his progress by its approximation of or proximity to Whites. Where there are no Whites, he or she will introduce them in ideology and/or fact.

This preoccupation is noticeable even among many who claim Afrocentrism as their philosophy. Caught up in an uncritical, racially based espousal of non-Whiteness as a definition of good and Whiteness as a definition of evil, such people apply racial characteristics to abstract qualities and emotions. Without Whites and a with romanticized view of ancient Africa, many Afrocentrists would have absolutely nothing on which to base their philosophy.

Any philosophy that causes African Americans to focus outside of the self for salvation is essentially escapist, and in that regard there is no philosophy more escapist than modern American integration. A lot of us give lip service to loving our Blackness, but when it comes to where and how we spend our money, and what our lifestyle, values, and aspirations are, almost all of us are haunted by "Whiteness." But this is not surprising because as we have moved to define ourselves as Americans., we are discovering that the ideal of being an American is to be(come) White or, at the very least, become acceptable to Whites.

For people of color, especially African Americans who have long struggled with our American identity, our search to actualize our self-concept is essentially a struggle to force Americans to redefine what it means to be American and for us to redefine what it means to be Black.

Actually, America is a Creole culture, a mulatto culture, a mestizo culture, and, especially in the arts, a predominately African American culture. If one views television, listens to the radio, and/or observes the night life of America with dispassion and honesty, one immediately notices the strength of African American influences. Yet, no matter how much Black speech is appropriated by advertising agencies and television personalities, the end result is that Whites are defining our existence. Listen to the background music.

Despite the various cultures that comprise this country, the economic and political control remains in the hands of those who identify themselves as Whites. Those African Americans who desire to have a profound impact on our destiny invariably find ourselves functioning in predominately White settings as we seek control of our communities. Although this struggle unavoidably must be waged against and among others, it is an internal struggle as well. Our internal struggle is to develop and accept our Black selves in the here and now as opposed to a romanticized Africa. Essentially, we must function with a double-consciousness, the same double-consciousness that DuBois wrote of so eloquently in *The Souls of Black Folk*.

Increasingly, African Americans are getting hip to integration. We know it has failed, and we are in the midst of a search for an alternative. That is the inner meaning of our focus on Malcolm X in the early 90s. Alas, this is not 1970. The current fascination with symbols of Africa, Nelson Mandela, Malcolm X, and sampling funk records from the 60s and 70s, although indicative of the search for roots, is no substitute for a coherent ideology of struggle. Moreover, it is not just our people who are at a crossroads in search of direction. America is also at a crossroads, and once again, the future direction of race relations will be made by the majority of Americans. The difference this time is that (within the next ten years or so) unlike in the 70s, the majority of Americans will not be White—they will be people of color.

No historically grounded African American would believe for one minute that all this discussion is happening because of a national concern about our social conditions. Time and time again, America has ignored our plight. No, there is another ghost rattling in the American midnight: White's fear of genetic and cultural annihilation. Whites fear being engulfed by an undammable rising tide of people of color washing onto American shores or reproducing in unchecked quantities. Frances Cress Welsing has been at the forefront in articulating this White fear of genetic annihilation.[13]

The failure to assimilate African Americans, or as some would say, to eradicate the poverty that is destroying African Americans, combined with the specter of more and more people of color literally overtaking America, is a sobering reality for all who think of America in typically White terms. This irreversible and inexorable "coloration" of the American

---

13. *The Isis Papers: The Keys to the Colors*, Chicago: Third World Press, 1991.

social landscape—the literal end of Whiteness as the majority definition of America—is the ultimate driving force behind all these concerns about multiculturalism.

Remember Bo Derrick validating braids as an acceptable hair style? For that matter, Madonna and Vanilla Ice did more to make rap acceptable to the mainstream than did any African American rap artist. And that is precisely the central failing of Black espousal of integration as it is practiced in America: African Americans not only end up pushing for White-defined acceptance, but Whites become the sole and/or main validators of what is acceptable. This vanilla validation process extends to defining African American culture.

We have bought into mainstream Americanism so deeply that we do not even realize the great American secret: we made America a democracy. Left to Whites, the ideal of American democracy would have remained a patriarchal, racist, and sexist ideal. The country would have been divided into a race-based Confederacy and a class-based, Federation. Only after the Civil War did America develop Jim Crow (North American apartheid).

The struggles of our people gave real definition to freedom and democracy. We forced America to be America. And today, it is in our interest to move beyond a fascination with integration. We must struggle to force America to be what it actually is, a country of color, rather than what it aspires to be, a bastion of White supremacy. The real integration would be to force America to accept its color, rather than to force people of color to accept ideological Whiteness.

Sun Song XI

kwanzaa: the drive to survive & develop/be yrself

i. umoja / unity
first, let's get together & do something
do something for self cause we want to we need too, in fact must,
cause if we don't, if we don't do it it won't get done
& in order to do, it takes at least two, really usually three
or more, maybe four, five, a couple of hundred, could even be
a band of twelve of us round some fire or a thousand on the move
but in order to go anywhere, we got to go as a we
not as a he or a she but a we & of course there are orders of unity
start w/the self (as in get yrself together) and move through
the family (family as in extended, not as in nuclear, not just blood,
but shared struggle & love, on thru community, the circle
of shared values, and race & nation, but not stopping there, must
keep on pushing and eventually get to the world, must be bold
and make the whole world filled w/a vision which includes
our sight lines, our sounds, our dance, our us, not afraid
to stand shoulder to shoulder w/everyone else and sing our own key
adding to the song of humanity, we are the blk angels
w/out our song there ain't no reel music in the world,
unity from self to the world starting w/the single soul vibrating
on the one right on out to anyone everyone any tone every
thing that exists can be got with, we can even dance
w/the devil & not get burned if we know that the purpose of unity
is to raise and to become lively upped, not to imitate and become

like the other, but rather to raise the whole, to elevate life
& suggest inside this blue brown circle of one, this planet
of life there is room for all if we move as one

ii. kujichagulia / self determination
self determines the nation, all the selves, each it's own head,
thinking abt life, deciding or declining to be/come part of the whole,
looking at down and figuring out how to get up, the only thing
you need to be told is "go for what you know, & be wise
which is to pass on what you got & cop what you ain't got, teach
what you know & learn what you don't, distribute the knowledge
& gravitate toward whatever you need to know that you ain't figured
out yet" i.e. think / do, be / come, arrive / leave, attain /
elevate, it is so obvious that we all have the capacity to do for self,
but what is not obvious is that we all have a significant contribution
to make to the motion of human history, not obvious because
we are so used to someone elses be calling the shots & we be
at best cheerleaders jumping up & down screaming bout them
"you got the ball, nah take it an run" but we don't be the ones
running nothing, or maybe we be sitting on the bench listening
to the white coaches relaying orders from the white owners
while we slurp hot dogs in the stands arguing abt which team is our team,
we ain't got no team, team, until we create ourselves
into a self determined force, and not just a twenty mule team either,
satisfied w/playing in their league by their rules, but a whole
human face body with eyes mouth and anus, arms and legs torso and
ears heart body and soul able to fully function and choose life and
choose life forms and social orders and not just be consumers
of some body else's constitutions, the only inalienable rights
are the ones we refuse to let anyone exercise for us on our
behalf on our ass, which means like to say from picking our colors
to the cut of our threads, from preparing the food we eat, to
choosing our friends and figuring out our enemies, from raising

the race, to elevating the planet, it is on us to paint the friendly skies,
in fact to make the skies and the ground more friendly, we
at the cross roads, it is on us to decide for us selves
which way to go to navigate and steer our own star ships

iii.   ujima / collective work & responsibility
doing it together is the simplest value there is, altho we understand that
our twisted condition may not be all or even mostly our fault, that we
in the shape we in because of others but it sho nuff is our responsibility
to get out the trap the others have set on us, you know we have to respond
to evil, response is human and righteous response to evil is important,
we have to respond, responding is a responsibility, how can we call ourselves
human if we let inhumanity be the order of the day, there is some work,
some tuff tuff kazi to be done, & whether we want it or not we are
batting clean up, we are the ones who must erase the graffiti anglo saxon
white supremacist slogans covering our souls, we must repurify the air
after foul industrial farts, we must distill the sewerage and chemically
tinged water, clean up the litter of capitalism & raw individualism run amok,
yes, and it will be hard, hard, very hard but that's why collective voluntary
associations of workers taking responsibility to respond to the damage
that has been done to the planet and to all the inhabitants of color
worldwide is necessary, true we have all been victimized, sullied
by being downpressed and colonialized, abused and misused, sucked
by bankers and merchant vampires and pimped and prostituted by a system
that likes our behinds but got no use for our minds, we know
we have been hurt by being brought here, being bought and sold here,
we know the trees are crying just like us, we know we are driven crazy
drinking cheap whiskey & wine, dropping drugs down our throats, we know
we been hurt, be hurting, all of a little dazed and confused and guess
what yall, the real reason we need ujima is cause can't none of us
transcend alone, not by ourselves, only in conjunction, hooked up
with our other selves, with the ying and yang of us, the seed and earth,
the male vibration and the female formation, so then like dancing on one foot,

it won't be true until we get on both good foots, until we do it
in cooperation, the healthy state is the embrace, when you hurting
you need a friend, a fellow worker, a comrade, a cut buddy, a lover, a
true blue, a collective so that when one itches, the other scratches,
having been slaves for so long the only way to save ourselves is to collect
our miserable pieces of selves together and holler
harambee, harambee, harambee

iv. ujamaa / family & cooperative economics

well don't you know somebody going to make the dough, so why not us,
we plow the fields so why can't we own the harvest, we make the music
so why somebody else got the license and pay us 12% royalties
when & if they feel like it, telling us our last million seller didn't
do so well, and after all expenses, we can expect to see a $38.94 check
in the mail sometime next year, economics ain't about nothing else but
who got the power to set the prices and print the money, indeed, to
declare what will be legal tender and what will be illegal commerce,
where you go to get the permit to sell the stuff you made, check that,
you got to go to somebody to get a permit to sell something you
made, is that real economics or is that exploitation mystified and
misidentified as a free market, where's the freedom when they got
the sons & daughters of slavery paying taxes to the same government that
enslaved our ancestors? in the year 2190 people gon wonder about us, wonder
what was wrong with us, wonder could we figure, you know what I mean, could
we add and subtract, wonder why it took us so long to set up our own
economy, our own system of the ownership, production, distribution and
consumption of goods and services, ah, pity the poor negro, a mouth trained
to eat the system's bull crap and pay through the nose for it at the same time,
and make no mistake cooperative economics is not capitalism painted black,
is not a beige-wahsee sitting in for the bourgeoise ramming pink toes
up our behinds, telling us that we are moving on up as they lift our coattails
to pick our pockets and ask us in an insulting fashion to celebrate enterprising
black capitalism that is pale (and generally ineffective) imitation of

*the legalized thievery which is the bane of the world, we need cooperative
economics, we need to cooperate with the earth, cooperate with other peoples
in the world, make sure that we all eat, we all healthy, we all sheltered
and clothed and that the richest live in the same part of town as the poorest,
that until there are no paupers there can be no millionaires, there
is no true economics without ethics, life is an ethical question not just
individual aggrandizement, no living large except to the degree that there is room
for all, fahamu, understand, there must be an economic vector to our struggle,
but an economics of ethics, cooperative economics, ujamaa*

v. nia / purpose
*we got a reason for being here, there must be a reason why,
always make the rational choice, keep the purpose in mind and the trip will be
worth the cost of the journey, do you know why you were born, was it just
a cosmic accident, oh no, the creator wasn't playing, wasn't just tossing loaded
dice upside the wall of reality, each one of us was born with both the potential
and the purpose of making this world better and more beautiful, and those of
us born black have a special duty to spread love and beauty which is what we do
better than anything we do, be beautiful at everything we do especially when
we do it from the heart, it is so obvious that we are roses, black roses in
the people garden, and orchids and violets, african violets, prettifying
and aroma-rizing the whole planet making everybody smile as we pass they way
smile, dance, sing, laugh, you know we can do that, & even though many
of us take our grace for granted, don't think too much about beauty,
be overlooking our ability to make peoples happy and saying like
what we really needs is rocket scientists and smart ass lawyers
sharp accountants and more businesslike black professionals who can beat
the man at his own game, but our purpose is higher than the bottom line,
our purpose is to raise, to levitate, to ascend, to make it hip, healthy & happy
to be human, and this only we can do, we have the soul to teach america
that there is nothing better than love, human beings loving and being together
with each other, nothing better than love and creating all the things we need
to be able to love each other, this is the gift of blackness: the ability
to keep the soul alive and happy, and what a gift, what a gift*

*love, health & happiness is, which is what we offer, give thanx & praises
and don't ever diminish or ignore the importance of making this world
better and more beautiful*

vi. kuumba / creativity

*even in a blizzard, every snowflake is different, which is all creativity is,
an individual stamp on every human act, some people smile with one dimple, with
two dimples, with no dimples, a gap in the front tooths, a little down turn of
the lip, a deep crease in the cheek, look around and you see it, every body smile,
smile right now and look at each other, see each smile is got something unique
in it and that's creativity at work, creativity is not just being different
one from another, but each one having our own unique difference manifested
in everything we do, our own instantly identifiable different, plus
the most creative of us is so hip that after we have done something
don't even have to be there and people know we done done it, or see
us coming a block away and know our walk, or hear us sing and
even when they can't catch the song know it's pouring out our throat, or
look at a flyer and can figure it was doug or somebody singing w/a pencil
or pen like that, well you know from cooking gumbo, to sewing indian clothes,
to fixing old cars, remodeling a house, even running a city, we should
be teetotally creative, our biggest problem is when we be aping
somebody else, especially the style of our former slave masters,
when we be trying to run city government but be afraid to make it too black,
scared of what the others gon say, well, hey, if we ran the city as hip
as we run a second line, everybody wouldn't have nuthin' to say but "yeah,
you right, go head on with your bad selves," can you imagine a city
run like a social aid & pleasure club, yeah thas what a city should be anyway,
nothing but a living large social aid & pleasure club, social
in that its about the human condition, aid in that we help each other
where and whenever we needs help and always, always, always for pleasure,
and why not, why do something for the pain of it, our creativity takes hard
and makes it look easy, takes crooked and makes it into a hip curve,
takes flat and puts another dimension on it, aren't you tired of seeing tired*

*toro poo-poo passed off as good looking stuff when we all know these cities
is so ugly when we are excluded from architecture and neo-urban planning
can you imagine life without blackness, pretty uh dumb, dumb, dull huh?
life without our music, life without our food, without our joy, our beauty,
our walk, our talk, our rhythm beat dance, without, life without us, can't be,
can't be, we the alpha and definitely gon be the omega, i mean this is not
racial flattery but rather hard anthropological fact, the whole world is africa,
human life started there, all humans is african, got africa in them
and if they can't get to that it's only because they either ignorant or shame
of they african origins, so what we, in all our joyful splendor do is simply
remind everybody in the world of what it truly means to be human
(which equals being african), you damn right we primitive, africa is the first
home of humanity, where all humanity emanates from and everytime we shake
that thing all we be doing is steady reminding the world that the human
thing is an african thing, which is why the whole world relates to our music,
music per se ain't really no universal language, african creativity is
the universal, and once we recognize that fact then we can be proud to be
ourselves and can understand why others want to be like us, they can't help it,
it's in everybody's blood, we in everybody blood, so this creativity thing
ain't nothing but our charge sparking, kicking life over, turning energy
engines to keep life going zooming on a hip tip*

vii. imani / faith
*faith is the evidence of things unseen, the belief in the future when you
ain't got nothing in the present and a had past, uncertain signs and hearsay,
if we believe that life starts when we are born and stops when we die
then we have no faith in life, no faith in self and the regeneration of life,
no understanding that we ourselves are nothing but life after death, after
the death of our parents and our grandparents, and their parents before them,
we are life, after they died and we still alive we are what, yes, say it,
we are life after death, we are proof that you can't kill life,
you can kill individuals but you can't kill black life, even after slavery,
and generations from now, after this mouth and your hand are gone to dust, after*

we have given up our lease on the spirit form, after that there will be other
life, and no matter how low i go, been downpressed, what i really believe
in is life happy, healthy and moving on up, life on a up beat, what
we need is what the native americans teach, seven generations:
three back, three forward, stepping from where we at, seven
generations strong let my song be proud and strong,
three deep back from me let everything i do be a positive extenuation
of what they started and three circles forward from now
let our great-grand children be exceedingly proud of what we struggled to do,
of the legacy of love & struggle we laid on them, and both finally and firstly
in the here and now, in this the swinging middle of seven generations
let our lives bring honor to humanity, let people think of us and smile,
think about being like us just see us and go to feeling good all over,
seven generations three back say let me make you proud, three forward say
let me make you proud, and all us in the here and now, say let me make you proud
& no matter what ever else, i'm going to believe in my own capacity to
make seven generations proud, to make seven generations proud, my own capacity
to raise self, family, community, race, nations & world to the seventh power,
you've got the power, believe, all you go to do is do it, you've got the power
seven generations, seven principles

afterword(s)
first thing we do, let's get together, and always
be our red/green/black selves unfurled in the winds
of life a human flag saluting the sun as we move collected
hooked up in a wheel within a wheel rolling down life's hiways
making sure that everyone is taken care of always
with the purpose of making life fine, fine, fine
and always new, unique, hip because each of our
thumbprints is stamped somewhere on the era
we cruise through stepping with in time stepping mellow
step, no rush, cause we know that we got the time, are time,
we got the beat, the rhythm of life is us breathing on the one
and by the time we finishing building this house

and throw the back door open for the party in the back yard
the sun gone be what, gone be shining, gone be shining
shining, shining in our back door

i believe that
what better do we have to do with our lives
than to be fine black & beautiful
i believe that
what better do we have than to be our
african selves
than to touch the world
and each other
than to be us selves
i believe that

there is nothing better
than being
than being
than being
yrself

Where Do We Go From Here?

Theoretically, America is a democracy—majority rule and all that. Actually, America is a oligarchy ruled by an interlocking nexus of corporate interests and moneyed families. In fact, the majority of Americans do not vote, but even if they did, the control of the country would not change hands.

During the 70s when African Americans waged liberation struggle, we really believed we were going to win. At the very least, we believed we would fundamentally alter the relationship between our people and our historic oppressors/exploiters. We did not win. We did make fundamental changes; however, the dominating system ultimately was able to accommodate a degree of fundamental change. Unfortunately for us, those changes did not alter the foundational balance of power.

Yes, there is a big difference between pre- and post-civil rights America. No, we have not improved our collective lot as a people. While numerous experts have pointed to the problem, precious few workable and effective solutions have been offered. The real question remains: Where do we go from here?

The solution must include economics as a major vector. While economics is not the bottom line of our struggle, without economics, there can be no liberation. No Black revolution can grow out of the barrel of a gun. Therefore, we must re-evaluate how we will make a revolution. I have always believed that our people will provide the answer to our problems. We just need to get a full understanding of where people are and what they want.

Without question, Blacks need economic power. Rather than pursue the traditional avenue of economic advancement in America (entrepreneurship), the "best and brightest" of our people have spent a great deal of time, effort, and resources trying to fit into the existing corporate economic structures. But if the best of us are working for the major corporations, where will our entrepreneurs and economic infrastructure come from?

Yet, we can not participate in economic competition until we have effected a political revolution. The problem with this is that politics in America is controlled by economics; and if we have no economic clout, we have no hopes of winning any significant political struggles. Politics without economics is prostitution.

The rather dismal and discouraging record of Black politicians during the 80s bears out the limitations of African American political struggle at all levels from community activism and parliamentary politics to warfare and post-war alliances and coalitions. We have been unable to affect politics beyond participation in and corruption by the mainstream. In fact, one well-known but seldom-acknowledged reality of our political struggle is that the vast majority of it was financed by philanthropic interests outside of the Black community.

A current possible solution is what I call horizontal economic development at a mass level in a specific economic sector. The traditional vertical mode of economic development is simply individual wealth generated by climbing the earnings ladder in a given field. The miscellaneous array of athletes and entertainers celebrated in Ebony and Black Enterprise are a prime example of this in our community. These individuals are excelling in mainstream pursuits that do not translate into well-being for the larger community.

What we need is a product we produce or a service we offer that would be uniquely associated with our people. From there, we could gain economic control of a specific market, from production to distribution to retailing. We need our own "Chinese restaurants." The product or service must have a broad appeal that is not localized, regionalized, ethnicized, and it must be one for which exists a national and international market.

As complex as the problem appears, the solution is both simple and obvious: African Americans must make a concerted effort to carve out a significant niche in the entertainment industry, specifically the music business area. I suggest music for three reasons: (1) it is a broad-based area that can allow for maximum involvement by individuals and organizations who do not necessarily have to be musicians; (2) it is lucrative and has a national and international market; and (3) it is an area where we can compete substantively.

Not only are there a wide array of musical genre possibilities available for African Americans' involvement (pop, jazz, blues, gospel, rap, etc.), more importantly, involvement in the music business is available beyond the actual production of music. Lucrative opportunities exist in direct support (management, bookings, engineering, sound reinforcement, etc.), as well as support in indirect areas (insurance, venue management/ownership, concessions, transportation services, printing, product manufacturing, etc.). Additionally, there are the ancillary operations such as publicity and media relations, which can range from publications to radio and video operations.

In 1983, when I became the executive director of the New Orleans Jazz & Heritage Foundation, Inc., I quickly discovered the lucrative nature of the music industry, which is lucrative to most involved — except for the musicians. The bulk of the industry is owned, managed, and operated by non-African Americans. As popularly noted, "show business" means we provide the show while they control the business.

While it is popular to talk about Jewish control of the music business, it is entirely misleading to single out Jews or anyone else as dominating the industry. Sure, a significant percentage of people who buy, sell, and broker our music are Jews, but the real point is that African Americans are not in charge and we ought to be. Our fight is to get in, not to put others down because they are already involved.

It will take a major struggle for us to gain significant footholds in the music industry, yet our chances of success are much greater in this industry than in any other. Yes, many Whites will fear and fight against a significant increase in African American control of the music business, but this is a battle that we are going to have to fight regardless of what area we venture into.

While we will catch flak from some, we will also receive support from others. Especially on an international level, the world is ready to deal with African Americans in the business side of music. In fact, many people in other nations have long wondered what is taking us so long to make this move.

One of the major advantages of an emphasis on the music industry is that our people can get involved from where they are and where their interests are. Furthermore, one does not necessarily have to be in any one specific profession. If on no other level, African Americans can begin to make personal financial investments to foster our people's development of control of the music industry.

Most people have no real appreciation of the full extent of the music business. For example, every music event in a major venue must have insurance. To my knowledge, no African American insurance companies are routinely contracted to provide insurance for musical events, yet, literally thousands of such insurance contracts are consummated on a monthly basis. Moreover, the risk factors are relatively small; very few of these policies are called on to cover the cost of an accident or insured incident. Similar opportunities exist in numerous other music-related areas. The point is that the music business affects so many areas of business that are non-musical. It offers the broadest array of opportunities for a diversity of skill areas while remaining focused in a particular economic sector. And this is the sector in which we African Americans can bring the greatest clout to bear. While we must create African American owned record companies, management companies, and the like, we also must understand that all of us do not have to work directly with music in order to benefit from and gain access to economic development in the music sphere.

Because of the potential clout of African American musicians, we as a people could significantly influence the selection of African American vendors of music-related products and services. The first step is to talk up the concept, spread the word, and get people excited about the idea. The second step is to encourage those of us in the industry to actively support the principle of using African American vendors for music-related goods and services. The third step is for African

American musical artists to exert specific pressure and demand (or insert the stipulation into their contracts) that African American vendors be used in support of their work.

None of this will take place over-night, yet the music business is one of the few segments of the modern American economy in which we have any significant leverage. Additionally, the music business is also one of the few business sectors in which an overwhelming majority of African Americans have an emotional investment. We love music regardless of our profession or aspirations.

The real challenge of integration is to capture control of economic development. We are the creative labor of a significant portion of the Black music industry. Now is the time to become the controllers of the fruit of our labor. African Americans desperately need economic development and a move on the music industry is a feasible route. We make the music. Now, let's make the money. Ideological and moral concerns such as what kind of music we should make and what messages that music should convey are questions that we need to address regardless of whether or not we gain economic control. Political struggle within the existing American system becomes irrelevant if one has no economic control. Music may be the only viable avenue available to us as a people. Until we have a better plan, let's get to swinging at seizing our music.

Sun Song XII

can we answer the challenge of year 2000
can we survive till then / be us selves till then
can we be we?
be Black (the basic African-Black
of us transformed by time on the cross
into the norf-nordic-american mutated
blue-black/brown/beige/tan/hiyellow of us
the northern edge upswing of the western hemispheric
diaspora dispersed like dandelion puffs
trade wind blown out of africa
and deposited by slavery onto plantations
and into other spaces of involuntary servitude
all the way from canada to chile)
?

can we sankofa?
retrieve & retain our cultural selves
carry us on past, the eighties, past the nineties
not just 98 or 99, nor 99&1/2 that just won't do
we gotta make a hundred new flowers bloom
into the first ray of new sunrise two thousand years
after european world domination: our struggle is
cultural survival post-colonialism, don't just want
to be here occupying space, consuming products and precious air
raising the ratings for overrated positive value-void videos

which mainline system sugar-shit suggestions into our
once wooly heads now chemical warfared into fried vacuums,
don't laugh, not many people have survived columbus' coming
into their faces, into their spaces, carrying capitalism to the
furtherest edge of every known world, cholera-coloring
every human impulse of generosity and welcoming,
where are the maya, the sioux, the cheyenne, the arawaks, the
aztecs, the original bajans, the people who used to carve wooden
turtles in the northwest, build adobe in the desert
collectively deliberate in long houses by the great lakes
and scientifically irrigate significant sectors of South America?

native culture does not survive capitalism unless it is
all the way 100% anti-white supremacy and just as strongly
unapologetically pro-self, anti-great god money & totally unimpressed
with the silly fickle bitch of popular success, able
to ignore tall buildings at a single glance and hiply
un-infatuated with air conditioning, naw, indigenous culture
facing horatio algier or michael jackson, for that matter, is
as useless as a quarter horse on a speeding freeway, unless it is
lightnin' hopkins wise, taking the stage after a white stage hand
has tuned his guitar, sitting down cool on the stool and
re-tuning his instrument, quietly saying to all assembled
within the sound of his amplified voice: "a guitar ain't tuned
'less you done tuned it tuned yrself! check that, you can't do nothing
unless you do it yrself, you (or no one else) can do anything
unless you do it yrself! and then lightnin' grins and swings
makes up some magically majestic music on the spot, music
so strong the arcing beam of the spotlight bends
and sweat on yr face feels freezing cold, culture can't survive
lessen we shape it up ourselves in our own image for our own
purposes in our own keys, can't survive unless
we jazz, forced into the atmosphere with the ferociousness
of bird&diz, klook&bud w/mingus playing notes so fast

the "cool schooled musicianers" couldn't even hear those notes
much less play them, unless you be max roach saying
"we wanted to play what the whites could not" not out of some
racial animonsity but out of self
awareness that we can be badder than anything standing here
if we would but challenge ourselves to out create capitalism,
come up with something so deeply meaningful that a 77 year-old
man who been beat down all his life would straighten up,
walk up main street past his boss dressed in white sheet,
past patrol car with dogs hanging out the window, past
the mayor's wife spitting at him, straight up into
sheriff taylor's acne pitted, pork fed, flushed, red face
and announce loud enough for the whole wide world to hear
that he intend to "regissss" so as he can vote
for the first time in his life, this is thursday noon,
it was wednesday night he was standing in the church, standing
in a circle shouting out the front part
of his snaggle-toothed mouth (and meaning every word of it)
that he "shall not be moved" cause he gon let his "lil light
shine" and shine, and shine so shiny it be blinding racism
and making the klan back down or at least think twice about
trying to scare these niggers who ain't scare no mo
we better be able to sing that song he sang, better at the very
least know that song when we hear it, better learn it and pass
it on to our children, cause it ain't the father, it ain't
the son, it's the holy ghost, yall, it's the spirit what
brung us on thus far and the spirit what gon carry us on

you don't have to be born again to believe in mahalia's music
just got to live the life you was given, understand
cause mahalia's moan can make a caterpillar butterfly
and that's all the matter with us
we need a cultural cocoon to develop ourselves in
and then we can fly out and be something real and beautiful, laugh

if you want to but ray charles & john coltrane have
done more to make america livable than indoor toilets
and refrigerator-freezers cause they pass spiritual nourishment
through us, and furthermore it ain't even no chance thing,
you can buy any coltrane record (whether you can dig it or not),
cop any trane record you can find, get it and it's bad,
guaranteed bad, this is culture
and this is the boat that will carry us
on to the other side even when all the bridges been burnt,
can't make your way through the maze of capitalist merchandising
unless we be like young mr. wynton marsalis certified able
to play everything europe has ever put on paper and then
turn around and blow rings around that stuff, understand he
is not bi-cultural, he is Black and because he Black he can deal
with everything happening in america today, listen to him
"jazz is the nobility of the race put into sound; it is the
sensuousness of romance in our dialect; it is the picture of the
people in all their glory..." skain don't you be so mean, but see
wynton is cultured, he has studied and taken himself, his history
seriously, his mentors are god men, deities like monk, armstrong
and ellington, listen to duke: "My men and my race are
the inspiration of my work. I try to catch the character
and the mood and feeling of my people. The music of my race
is something more than the American idiom."—that phrase bears
repeating: "The music of my race is something more
than the American idiom." and then Duke continues: "It is
the result of our transplantation to American soil
and was our reaction, in plantation days, to the life we lived.
What we could not say openly we expressed in music.
The characteristic melancholic music of my race
has been forged from the very white heat of our sorrows
and from our gropings. I think the music of my race
is something that is going to live,

something which posterity will honor
in a higher sense than merely that of the music of the ballroom."
end of quote. compare that statement to the latest press release
from the last negro politician you voted for

can we sankofa? can we catch up with our older selves
can we be conversant with what was the word in 1886 right after
we had picked up arms and marched shooting cross dixie
forever altering the image of the docile neggra,
can we quilt our history, i mean take all the little
pieces, the tattered rags, the torn dresses, the slashed
jackets whipped off our backs, the cotton sack smocks, the
flour sack shirts, the pieces of cotton we spun and
made curtains with, the little overpriced pieces of lace
we purchased with hard saved money and put on our mother's heads
for third sunday communion, the colorful bits of ribbon
braided bodaciously into a child's hair as she is sent off
to face the animal wrath of white inhumans trying
to hold on to segregation, can we research us selves,
gather bit by bit, even though we can't remake a whole
no more out of what is left of us after auction block,
after language strip, after dignity rape, but still take
all the strips and left-overs, and shorts-bits,
hidden scraps of our humanity we've balled up and salvaged,
so what we do when the puzzle can't be pieced back together,
what we do is make a quilt, and that quilt is our history
is how we will have to get ourselves together, what we will use
to protect us from the cold and beautify our intimate
spaces at the same time, so you walk into our space and
immediately know you are in our space, its up to us to
form sewing circles: the quilt is our cultural pattern

somebody besides aliens needs to write the history of sncc
in every city there needs to be a music society bent
on salvaging memorabilia, paraphernalia, posters & flyers

old records & ticket stubs, photographs & instruments,
costumes & uniforms too, needs to be cataloging all the
old records, the 78's and the cylinders, somebody should
give us anthologies of poetry taken from negro newspapers and
church bulletins from the twenties, what about having an
old Black picture day and collecting every picture
of anything blood was doing, or being, or looking like, or
looking at, and each city coming out with big picture books
and making them books mandatory in public school (which
all across the country is the new penal colonies for
young Blacks), people be talking bout crack and AIDS,
but ignorance gon take us completely out of the game
if somebody don't understand that culture is the calabash
within which the soul is carried, and bodies without soul
is just flesh, just flesh, hemoglobin and tan meat,
if somebody don't peep the need to preserve culture,
to be bad in year 2000, to be Black and bad, to be African
to be Africa more than a memory, a game preserve and a
place for rich whites to vacation, to be alive and human
with five fingers on each hand, five toes on each foot
and relatively healthy, not eaten by cancer, limbs missing
incurable diseases blighting our genes, to be alive and
reaching out to the world offering inventive manipulations
of post chattel-slavery, post reconstruction,
post-segregation, post-negro-mayors, post-white domination
of our minds, to be offering alternative vision
and making that into modern quilts, why else be here, why else
even run the race into the future, why else live
if we can't be Black, bad and Black
and at least as hip as our enslaved ancestors
who created us and created the only people's culture
to survive capitalism?

that is the challenge of year 2000!

Back to the Bush

T he trajectory of my life history informs my every thought and colors each emotion I manifest.

Once you have been out there a minute, regardless of how far out (or how far in) your "out there" is, the resulting thoughts and feelings generated while passing through your experiences are always a part of you. Even when you reject some particulars of the whole, the experience remains—attracting or repulsing the arrow of your internal compass.

We may forget, but we cannot erase. Our emotional color is a patina, enriched or enviscerated by the weathering of existence.

Intuitively our folk have always understood the importance of the vessel. Thus we carved into the side of the calabash before we drew the water. We painted the walls, inside and out, before we lived in the shelter. Likewise, with our lives, to live creatively is the crucial aspect of Afrocentricity. Unfortunately, as humans, we often fall prey to the great conceit that it is thought alone that elevates us to the highest status in "god's creation." In the process of thinking so much, we often do not understand that thought itself is just a lever. We do not understand that the essence of what makes us who we are is not solely or even mainly thought. Indeed, the "us" of us often exists independent of whatever thoughts our brains may have.

From this perspective, we can begin to understand that the whole of us is a synergistic totality that we ignore at our peril. We are body&soul. Each of us possess mind (thought), body (sensation), spirit (soul), and consciousness (will).

Those of us who struggle for change often lean so heavily on our thoughts that ideas become crutches and obfuscations to living a meaningful life. We often end up more enamored of ideas than people, more ready to think about something than to touch someone. Although once you start thinking it is hard to stop, the majority of us do very little deep thinking, not to mention deep feeling, deep (spiritual) being, or deep willing (practicing heavy manners or exercising self-discipline).   In fact, the deepest thinker is the person who knows both how to think and how not to think.   This "objective knowledge" is incomplete, indeed, impossible without making use of the whole of self: head, heart, gut, and gonads.

While thoughts may give directions, feelings generally dominate and dictate. When feelings dictate, thoughts serve. We live in the 20th century, a so-called rational age; yet our gonads often govern us far more than our minds. A taste for something dictates the way home or the way away from home. Desire is an incredibly strong force in most of our lives.

Our attitudes toward struggle, each other, love, child-rearing, the foods we eat, employment, education, religious orientation, ethical systems, and more are harnessed in the sling of our emotions—no matter how much we think about our actions. However, emotions are not abstract entities, unshapable, unmalleable, unchangeable givens; like thoughts, like everything that exists, emotions change and are changeable. Not unlike most people, the majority of my emotions have been profoundly affected by the behavior modification of lessons learned both consciously and subconsciously as a result of my being here including how I was born, how I have lived, how life has treated me, and how I have treated life.

I have always believed that the physical environment as well as the social environment is a major factor in establishing the emotional personality. Like the old folks say, you can judge a person by the company they keep. This includes one's physical and environmental as well as social company. Therefore, I listen to our music far more than I watch television, videos, and movies combined. There are art and photographs in all the spaces in which I live and work. I read books and magazines more than newspapers and pop novels. I don't "hang out" and tend to be very, very selective about the time I spend in other people's company. I don't think I'm better than anyone else, or that I'm right and others are wrong. I know I am essentially just like everyone else. The point is that I am on a mission, and a major aspect of that mission is to develop myself as an alternative to the mainstream. Like most fanatics unalterably dedicated to a specific ideal, I've drawn little "lines in the sand" to mark out my psychic "territory" and to declare my partial independence from the status quo.

For example, one of the lines I have drawn in the sand, the line that, in effect, circumscribes my mission, is my refusal to ever again wear a suit and tie. I think of the suit and tie as the costume of 20th-century imperialism. Yet, I don't make a fuss about this. This is my personal line in the sand and not a measuring stick for everyone else. There are many people who are fighting for change who wear suits and ties everyday. So I do not mistake a personal preference for a collective political statement, nor do I judge others based on my own personal choices. Nonetheless, I know it is important for all of us to define ourselves and, in defining ourselves to define the mode and manner of our daily behavior that resultantly shapes our emotional responses and proclivities. It is important that we draw lines and set the limits of what we will tolerate. Far too much of our oppression exists because we accept the oppressive behavior of others. Part of being free is continuing to struggle against enslavement.

We can all learn to be better people than we are, just as we learn to pretend we enjoy the taste of alcohol when it's really the effect of alcohol on our nervous system that we truly enjoy. Most people who drink disguise the taste of the alcohol by mixing their drinks or by buying drinks that have flavorings added. In a similar way, people tend to disguise their true emotions and thoughts by adding extraneous flavors, which are often put forward as the given reason for a commitment or non-commitment. These flavors actually conceal the real reasons and motivations. I have spent a great deal of my life trying to get to the real, trying to eschew facades and flavorings.

I do not think I am fundamentally different from anyone else in terms of how I function. I think deep down most of us want to get next to the real us, and that is essentially what "living in the bush" means—getting to the internal, real us and building on our personal, collective, and environmental potentials.

The hard part is that the real us is a changing us, not some mythical, specific ideal or destination. We may push forward toward an ideal or even retreat from it, but the ideal is not us. It is the motion toward or away from, the potential for further development and retardation, that is the real us. As we get older, it becomes increasingly difficult to distinguish what's real from what's peripheral, added on, expendable, and/or artificial. This is especially the case for those of us who have waged struggle to bring about fundamental change in this society. Regardless of the difficulty of this knowing, our ancient ancestors remained right on target when they declared the primal law of existence to be "know thyself!"

II.

I was in a recording studio recently and the pianist joked that he remembered me from when I took over the mayor's office.   He concluded that once they gave me a job at the Jazzfest, he had not heard a peep more from me. We both knew he was exaggerating, but the residual truth is that after that action I did in fact recede from the front lines of leading street demonstrations.

I was well into my thirties when I participated in a take over of New Orleans City Hall. I led a three-day sit-in at the office of the city's first Black mayor. The issue was police brutality. Within a period of twelve months, there had been thirteen killings by police all under very questionable circum-stances. It appeared the city administration was not going to deal definitively with the situation. There seemed to be open season on poor Blacks by the New Orleans Police Department.

Our response was to organize, agitate, and finally disrupt. It took so much. We had to deal with infiltrators, agents provocateurs, and the miscellaneous array of socially battered individuals who often cause more dissension internally than is healthy for any movement.

For example, once we held a rally in the chapel at Dillard University. Just obtaining the chapel for a rally site was a major accomplishment because Black college presidents in general historically have been much more conservative than militant in their social orientations.   In fact, within our ranks, there were a number of people who did not understand why we chose Dillard as our rallying site and/or did not agree to hold the rally there.   Yet, rallying at Dillard demonstrated the broadest possible support for our effort. I was under no illusions about the Dillard administration, however.

While our rally was going on in the chapel, two well-known community activists were squaring off in the bathroom, facing off for a serious throw-down. Somebody was going to get a royal ass-kicking. I was summoned to intervene. One of the brothers was a self-selected castigator of chumps, toms, lackeys, petit-bourgeoise, and sellouts—the possessor of a sharp mind and a wealth of information. He was one of the single most disruptive forces within our ranks. The other brother was a fiery, quick-tempered, Vietnam veteran who, although one of the most intelligent brothers in our movement, was just as likely to settle an argument with the quickness of his fists as with the articulateness of his mouth. As I stood between them—amidst wolf tickets thick in the air, half wishing for one to kick the other's ass, and at the same time aware of how destructive such infighting could be for our movement if it became a public affair—I realized just how slim the long-term chances of our success were.

By the time we made the move to take over city hall, we had actually had fist fights with each other and fortunately had managed to avoid shoot-outs. As imbecilic as the idea of self-styled revolutionaries killing each other may seem on the surface, such internecine warfare was actually the norm rather than the exception in all of the 20th-century movements I know of. It was neither less nor more the case in America.   In New Orleans, we were fortunate in avoiding an escalation of our fights to the level of homicide. We also discovered and expelled police infiltrators. We disciplined and/or rid ourselves of disruptive forces, some of them self-avowed "scientific" revolutionaries.

One group put out a "Death to the Klan" leaflet in our collective name, and then not only refused but indeed objected to any of us taking up arms to challenge the Klan when it announced it would hold an international Klan convention in the New Orleans area. At one point in preparation for dealing with the impending showdown with the Klan, we called a special meeting and set a criterion that a rifle was a prerequisite for attending; handguns were not acceptable. The "revolutionaries" showed up without arms because they thought we were joking. At a subsequent meeting, they were forcibly ejected. And they had nerve enough to be both surprised and emotionally hurt! Nonetheless, we moved on without them. When confrontation day came, those who called for "Death to the Klan" were actually sideline onlookers fearing a bloodbath. After that situation, it was hard for me to take seriously a lot of the "talk" that brothers do about revolution. Also, I learned that those who often pushed the hardest for "revolutionary" action were either infantile and/or infiltrators. When it came down to actually putting their own bodies on the line and really making a commitment, they balked at armed struggle. Paradoxically, that demonstration also marked the beginning of the end of one phase of my life.

The demonstration itself was boldly successful. The Justice Department and FBI sent in agents who tried to persuade us not to hold the demonstration. We ignored them. Also, we made clear in a press conference that the two bodies—us and the Klan—could not occupy the same space at the same time. At high noon we intended to be in full effect.

If some stuff went down, we indicated that the Klan was not going to be the only ones shooting, and we were not going to be the only ones dying. The Klan folk changed the time of their demonstration.

From these events and others, I learned two important principles: (1) once we set our people in determined motion, the system will make some adjustments, generally minor but sometimes major, in order to keep itself in place; and (2) real revolution, an actual change of political power and economic control, is still a long way off. In hindsight, this last point may seem as obvious as heat on a summer day. But back then—especially in the early 70s, incredulous and/or ludicrous as it may seem—we actually believed and acted like revolution was but a year or two away.

We at Ahidiana had our whole organization (including our young children) on the street for that demonstration. Although we had the good sense not to flash our weapons, nearly everybody in the crowd was packing heat, and there were several carloads of weapons strategically located at the rally site. The city police as well as state and federal forces knew the deal, which is why they got the Klan to back down from its announced time of high noon. They escorted Klan members in to the Klan's rally site at 8 a.m. and escorted them out before 9 a.m. They too wanted to avoid a showdown, not because they were concerned about Black people dying, but because they were concerned about the possibility of an all-out race war with both sides armed and prepared to kill and die. It was the largest demonstration of armed Black folk I have ever attended. We sent out the call and even the street people responded. Nobody messed with Black people that day.

But we caught hell keeping that militancy in motion. For

the Klan showdown, the enemy had been highly visible. There was a definite time, date, and place for the showdown, rather than weeks, months, and years of incremental and grueling organizing. Moreover, it did not call for protracted trench work, but one massive show of strength—a large number of people gathered who, for various and easily understandable reasons, were not ready, willing, or able to run the long distance of protracted struggle—but who had among them a significant percentage willing to make a do-or-die stand. However, the reality is that "high noon" does not come every day. Most days, revolution is a routine grind. For most of us, the grind was far from easy and did not, again for understandable reasons, include building an army to engage in day-to-day armed struggle. Our organization, Ahindiana, ran a school, a book-store, a printing press, a food co-op but not an army, nor did we have a militaristic bent.

Ours was a rhetoric and a reality of creating alternatives to the status quo, and toward that end we knew it was important to be visible in our community on a day-to-day basis. Yet, the effort required to construct that visibility and the prioritizing of resources necessary to sustain alternative institutions pulled us away from confrontational activity as a general tactic, even as the discipline of institution building prepared us for protracted struggle. By the time of the Klan demonstration, we had instituted teaching and weaponry practice for all of the adults (women and men) in the organization. We had no romantic notions about arming ourselves. Few people in the community even knew, but we were prepared.

Finally, the central contradiction boiled down to which route was more effective, aggressive confrontational organizing or all consuming institution building. There is much to be said for both sides of this argument. Within our organization, some of us were constantly waging a struggle against the conservatism inherent in institution building. When you put years into building a school, you are not inclined to jeopardize the school's existence just to confront a corrupt politician, especially when the confrontation is led by self-styled leaders whose most outstanding characteristics are talking loud and trashing others. On the other hand, institution building can also sometimes be used as a facile and ultimately cowardly argument for inaction that justifies non-confrontation for fear of losing what one has. We reject this same argument when we talk about "sellout" negroes who are afraid to lose their fat paychecks or lose access (actually proximity) to powerful people. Why should we expect others to give up what they have, what they have earned by whatever means, or even to simply give up their leisure time, if we are unwilling to give up what we have? Certainly, there is a big difference between sacrificing an up-scale third Mercedes and sacrificing an alternative educational institution. On an individual level, it boils down to the same basic sacrifice: giving up that which one ardently desires and has worked hard to achieve in order to demonstrate opposition to the status quo. Within Ahidiana, we spent many hours struggling with these issues. Nevertheless, on that day when it was time to face the Klan, we stood solid.

After standing on that front line at high noon, the many days, weeks, and months that followed were a horse of a different mule. The overall momentum to oppose the Klan had been put in place, not by a single organization but by a coalition of people. As is usually the case with crisis-based coalitions, the center could not hold beyond a single, issue-oriented activity. Indeed, once a significant number of people reach the level of mass armed struggle, the stakes quickly escalate. Particularly in America, Black people often find ourselves left with very little room to maneuver. Externally, all kinds of pressures are brought to bear, and internally, we experience a false euphoria and a bravado that wants to push us immediately to the next level. But what should follow after getting a populace to turn out for an armed demonstration?

In the days that followed that Klan showdown, I began to understand the often misunderstood and easily dismissed classic statement that is credited to Stalin—that is, when a movement reaches a peak it is both strongest and weakest; that when one became one's strongest, one is often also about to crack. Another way to put it is this: if you throw a ball in the air, it reaches its greatest height precisely when it runs out of force and is about to fall back to the ground. These are among the hard philosophical lessons that revolutionaries everywhere have had to understand when taking on seemingly invincible odds, when facing an overwhelmingly stronger opponent, and when forced to develop successful strategies to maintain the momentum of struggle.

Today, it is obvious to me   that people who spout revolutionary rhetoric but do not back it with revolutionary organizing and revolutionary study are not really revolutionaries. To think that agitating and demonstrating are synonymous with revolutionary movement is a farce. Self-proclaimed and self-deluded revolutionaries, no matter how serious, are actually only social dissidents and rebels protesting conditions in the status quo, rather than revolutionaries committed to seizing state power. The former essentially want a break, some relief from and repair of specific ills rather than a different form of government or economic system. In fact, most people have no clue as to what state power actually entails. We are simply dissatisfied with racism, with living under White people. If it were actually left up to many of us, we would end up duplicating much of what currently exists, just putting Black people in charge of it. And for me that was the major rub: recreating the status quo in Black face is not and never will be my goal.

On the other hand, I ask myself, what have we actually achieved? Although simply reforming the status quo was not my ultimate objective, reform has actually been the main result, at best, of the majority of my life's work. So part of what I have had to face is the glaring distinction between my revolutionary visions and my reformist results. Any honest assessment must speak directly to contradictions that often had little to do with fighting the racism of Whites and everything to do with questioning my own and my people's efforts and visions, questioning what we have done with what we have acquired.

For example, we at Ahidiana introduced Kwanzaa in the New Orleans community. We also made a conscious decision to turn over leadership of Kwanzaa to others because we genuinely wanted Kwanzaa to become a citywide celebration rather than be perceived solely as an Ahidiana event. Over a decade later, Kwanzaa is now acceptable on a mainstream level. Certainly, that is a victory.

But even as the awareness of Kwanzaa has grown stronger, the reality of African Americans actualizing and living the objectives of Kwanzaa are further away than ever. Moreover, the contradictions have heightened.* Nevertheless, it seems

---

* I was deeply saddened to witness one of the Kwanzaa spokespeople at a 1992 Kwanzaa celebration leading the assembled audience in a prayer "in Jah's name." Kwanzaa is not a religious holiday, nor should it be used by any religion to present itself to our community.

that genuinely progressive elements are in charge and that we have achieved what we essentially wanted.   However, the results are not what we wanted.   This experience is similar to that of various independent "Third World countries" whose revolutionary governments turned out to be far from effective in serving the needs of the people.   The officials of those governments, with a repetitious and seemingly perennial regularity that bordered on a 99% statistical mean, ended up being the greatest impediments to some of the most sacred goals of the liberation movement.

African Americans are a long way from real revolution. This was one of the realizations I had after we took over city hall.   The American system is so deeply entrenched in the psyches of our people. As we entered the 80s, although I had never shied away from confrontation, I knew the era of community protests was drawing to an end. If for no other reason, the status quo now had Black faces in high places to whom the majority of our people wanted to give a chance to make change. The 80s was the era of Black politicians, and you see what it got us.

As the fervor for 80s-style integration took hold, we 70s-era rebels who aspired to be revolutionaries scattered to the four winds, each faction of us just trying to maintain life and limb, trying to keep the wolves from our doors and the craziness out of our emotional lives. We did not all succeed.   Many of us went off the deep end and became militant agitators for reform or professional left-leaning social workers. Others of us went back to school, to jobs, to parents, and resigned from even thinking, talking, or being in the proximity of any kind of oppositional, not to mention revolutionary, struggle. Some of us could not stand the strain and had mental breakdowns. A much smaller number tried to continue our motion and quite a few former hardened revolutionaries "got religion." They literally became reverends, imans, or proselytizing, born again Christians. Essentially, what happened was that when we failed to make revolution on the ground, when we failed at systemic change, we went for the standard American fall-back position: internal revolution. We changed ourselves. Although many of us claim that we are still about revolution, the day to day focus of most of our present attempts at revolution narrow down to a focus on the individual and on the handful of people with whom we come into daily contact.

For others, the failure to fundamentally change the system meant that we had to regroup. Most often, we had nothing to replace the time, energy, dedication, and belief we had put into the liberation movement. Meanwhile, we all had lives to live, lives that demanded time and resources: spouses, spousal equivalents, children to raise and educate, bills to pay—the usual host of day-to-day elements that slow down most militants.

By 1983, when I left the *Black Collegian Magazine*—interestingly enough, two of my fellow staff members had to physically restrain me from jumping the newly appointed vice president of the magazine—I had consciously decided that I had run out of ideas about how to deal with New Orleans from an activist perspective. I honestly did not know how to counter the wave of false euphoria that people perceived a Black mayor was ushering in. I did not know how to maintain an alternative institution in the face of irreconcilable internal differences. I just did not know what to do.

I threw myself into my new job at the New Orleans Jazz & Heritage Foundation. I did a lot of behind-the-scenes and covert support work. The metaphor I used to describe myself at this stage is that of a field slave who has been selected to work in the big house yet who, once inside, tries to slip as much food as he can back to the people in the field. That too quickly grew frustrating because ultimately, the better I did my job, the more I built up the status quo. So in 1987, I quit and went to work full time for Bright Moments, a public relations and event production agency founded in 1984.

In partnership with Bill Rouselle, a brother whom I had known and worked with in struggle for almost twenty years, we envisioned Bright Moments as our way of being independent, of not working for anyone but ourselves. Personally, I also decided to spend the next five years of my life working mainly in the area of cultural production.

In the summer of 1992, I was pleased with what I had accomplished and, at the same time, more ready then anytime in the previous ten years to move to another level of activity. So here I stand at yet another crossroads: I have more work than I can realistically handle, I am always short on time, always pushing to complete a project on time as literally four or five other projects compete for resources and attention. During the last half of the 80s—although it was harder because I lacked resources and was living literally gig-to-gig as far as financial stability went—it was also easier because I often had literally no choices whatsoever but to press on.

Today, my life is different, and I suspect this difference is not simply one of degree. I think of drummer Chico Hamilton's record, *A Man from Two Worlds* (the one that featured saxophonist Charles Lloyd), I think of W. E. B. Du Bois' double-consciousness, Amilcar Cabral's analysis, his effort to be specifically African and generally human at the same time, and I look at the unique African American experience. I am African and American and trying to figure out how to synergize these identities without one overwhelming the other. What is the best way to strive for and achieve balance? That is my struggle and I sense this is the struggle of many other survivors of the 80s.

Some will argue that African Americans are neither legally nor emotionally Americans, that we are enslaved Africans, pure and simple. I reject this argument because it is usually an argument based solely on some false rationale or contrived explanation. The fact is the majority of our people have been changed to the core by the experience of being born, living, struggling, and dying in the United States of America. Whether we like it or not, agree with it or not, we are Americans. Indeed, the future definition, just like the history, of America is inconceivable without taking our people into consideration. This does not mean that I swallow the American line as it is cast by the ruling class; I am not a fish. It just means that half the story's never fully been told, and we, probably more so than White folks, will ultimately define the future of America.

CODA:

Becoming the Best of Both/Eye-self & We-self

Sun Song XIII

be about beauty
as strong as a flower is
yet as soft too
as an open petal
receiving the mist
of a midnight raindrop,
be about beauty
no matter life's dirt
be about beauty

To Be Continued

Individual material success means very little to me. Individual success does not put a song in my heart. It is difficult for me to see my people in sorrow: to drive to work past workless brothers leaning stagnant against the walls of abandoned buildings; to see our sisters moving against the wind, two children in tow, the eyes of each of the three of them older than all three of their chronological years combined; to observe the desperation and duplicity fouling the air anywhere near the municipal courts of law; to view the macho posturing of rappers influencing four-year-olds; to witness talented young Black women prostituting themselves in the name of making records, movies, and videos. If my people are not healthy, then I too am sick. Recognizing the depth and possible terminal nature of our sickness, I am convinced, more than ever, that we need a revolutionary cure.

However, there is a thin, thin line between keeping the faith and deluding oneself. I have been too close to revolution to use the word lightly. Besides my experiences in this country, I have gleaned many lessons from dialogue and struggle on other soils with other peoples. I took two trips to Cuba and engaged in hours of ideological struggle and sharing. * I was

---

* While in Cuba, I spent several days in the company of Assata Shakur, a genuine hero of our movement. Her autobiography ought to be read as extensively as a lot of people claim they have read Malcolm's.

in Suriname when an attempted coup went down. A state of siege under a militarist, so-called revolutionary government is no joke. Although it is true that power grows out of the barrel of a gun and that we will have to seize control if we are to truly get control, it is also true that the ethics of the finger on the trigger is the essential revolutionary question.

I visited China in 1977 and I was in Peking when Deng was rehabilitated. In China, after days of insisting on an ideological session, we finally had a meeting and for the first time it was clear that throughout our visit party thinkers had been presented to us. Then and there, I realized that no matter how egalitarian a revolution purported itself to be, there was always, always a group at the center who were at a significantly different level than the majority of the people who did the work. These guys looked differently, dressed differently and put forth a line that made it clear they did not fear a third world war. I wonder where these guys stood on the recent student rebellion which was so brutally crushed. But more than these party intelligentsia, I remember the young translator who avoided eye contact and dropped her head as she said "just follow the party line" when questioned about ideological reversals.

I can remember President Nyerere of Tanzania telling a small group of us that "all governments are conservative." He repeated and emphasized the word "all," referring to the tendency of bodies in power to do whatever is necessary to maintain their power. Years later, in the mid-80s, I was journeying by bus and ferry through war-ravaged Nicaragua. After two days of travel, including hours standing in the rain waiting, two of us finally caught the once-a-day bullet riddled ferry to complete the last leg of our trip. Early one Bluefields morning, we managed to have a brief interview with Ray

Hooker, a Black leader who had been captured and seriously wounded by the Contras. Hooker represented a third force, neither Contra nor Sandinista, a force that was seeking autonomy within the context of Nica.Libra independence. I heard gunfire in the hills at night, survived a few close scraps on the road back, and knew that what we cavalierly call revolution in the United States bears little resemblance to the disruption, death, and destruction that accompanies actual revolution. I have seen and talked with the refugees of war, the people who are always caught in the middle. My experiences do not allow me to play at revolution.

In Trinidad, a once oil-rich nation, I witnessed the ruination that wanton materialism can wreak on the psyche of a nation. Early in the 80s, in Haiti, I witnessed ruination that wanton poverty can wreak as well. I do not know which of these conditions is worse, but I am thankful I do not have to choose either. Yet, I am a victim of both. Many African Americans are almost as poor as Haitians are materially, while a significant number of us are as materially spoilt (spiritually impoverished) as some formerly nouveau-rich, now nouveau-poor Trinidadians.

Toward the end of the 80s, I found myself walking through the bleak winter streets of London seeking out South African revolutionary Wally Sarote, who was both a writer and a high-ranking party official in South Africa's ANC . This was years before Mandela's release was won. At that time, it seemed Mandela would remain a forever-imprisoned martyr. Bundled in the only coat I owned, I trudged for miles through the winding, haphazard streets. Finally, I found Sarote's flat. Although this was our first time meeting, the two of us chatted like old comrades. Our connection had been Willie (a.k.a. Keorapetse Kgositsile), a South African writer and ANC officer

whom we both knew and loved.   At this point, the Black
Liberation movement in South Africa was hurling unstoppably
forward while the movement in America was slowing to a crawl.
Yet, as I talked with Wally of drawing inspiration from the South
African struggle, Wally told me how much of an inspiration
African American struggles had been to South African militants
during their long night/long winter of repression.

At age forty-six, as I look back and forward, as I look
outward and inward, there are many miles under my feet.
Many ideas have run through my head, and both bitterness and
joy have a house in my heart. Regardless of contradictions and
victories, failures and accomplishments, regardless of how
many dues I have paid in the past, I know I must travel on.   I
cannot afford to stay weary when I do inevitably become weary.
Being Black here in America can make you so very tired. The
intense discouragement of specific days notwithstanding, the
seemingly lack of win in our game and despite all of the seeming
unending disasters on our Third World horizon, I will continue.

And even as I continue my journey through this world, I
believe that every step forward is truly progressive only if it
carries me further back into myself, my people, my history, the
world in which I live, back into the "bush"—the basic self, all the
elements that make us who we are. True progress never leaves
the past behind.   True progress is but an extension of the past
and is always, in essence, nothing but a better way for humans
to live with each other, the earth, and the elements. Those of
us who do not dwell deep in the bush of ourselves can never
go forward to the "promised land" because the real promised
land is not a destination, not a nation-state but an inner-state of
being, caring, sharing, and loving.

Regardless of what we gain or lose in the material sense, in the final analysis the quality of our lives boils down to relationships rather than acquisitions. The nature of our interconnectedness is much more accurate a gauge of individual and collective progressiveness than any conventional measure of economic or political power. At best, economics and politics should be but a means toward the end of creating a better society, as measured by the relationships of individuals within the society to each other and to the world as a whole.

Essentially, all of life is a constant transition between birth and death. The measure of one's life is how well one has lived in the social and environmental sense. I, as a non-theocentric spiritualist, believe in the basic karma of life rather than in any particular god or gods. When I die, I believe that I will return to wherever I was before I was born. Until then, I am responsible for setting in motion as much positive energy as possible and for curtailing as much negative energy as I can. By promoting the positive and combating the negative, I extend both the quantity and the quality of life for myself and for all others affected by my every life motion. Specifically, as an African American artist, my task is to document and inspire; to leave behind a record of who and what we are/were—what we felt, thought, believed, how we lived—and to inspire others to consider the profound importance of living a good life in one's own space and time.

To paraphrase Amilcar Cabral, I am but a simple African (American) man trying to live the best I can within the context of my own particular space and time. This may not be the best of times, but it is the only time I have, so I plan to live to the fullest while I am here.

Peace & liberation, love and understanding.